It's A Matter Of
Trust

David Batchelor & Dean Hobbs

It's A Matter Of Trust
by David Batchelor & Dean Hobbs

First edition published in December 2016:

Wills & Trusts IFP Ltd trading as
Wills & Trusts Chartered Financial Planners
91/92 High Street
Thame
Oxfordshire
OX9 3EH
Telephone 01844 212907
Facsimile 01844 261265

Paperback version printed and bound by Amazon CreateSpace

ISBN-13: 978-1541131996

WRITE BUSINESS RESULTS

This book was produced in collaboration with Write
Business Results Ltd. www.writebusinessresults.com
info@writebusinessresults.com

Contents

PART 3: Family

PART 4: The Practicalities

PART 5: Post Death

PART 6: Successful Estate Planning

In November 2016 we met with a couple, John and Lily, who wanted us to review their Wills to make sure they were up to date and would pass their estate to their children. The couple's Wills had been drawn up by a local solicitor. They were not married, but had lived together for 17 years and each had two children. In the event of either of their deaths they wanted the survivor to have everything, and then on the subsequent death, pass the full value of the estate to the four children equally.

The Will did exactly this. It passed the estate first to the other partner and then down to the four children equally. What the Will also did was to generate a huge tax liability, not only when one of them died, but to an even greater extent when the money passed to the children!

As the couple were not married, it meant that they had no 'spousal exemptions'. This meant that when John died and passed £500,000 to Lily, only £325,000 would be free from inheritance tax, creating a tax liability of £70,000. That's £70,000 that Lily would have to pay when John died.

When Lily then died she would have £1,000,000 to pass to the four children. She would have her standard tax free allowance as well as the new residential tax allowance from April 2017. But because John's children were not her children, the money that they received would not qualify for the new allowance. The result of this is that if Lily died in 2017, there would be an additional £230,000 due in inheritance tax.

Bad news, and certainly not what John and Lily had wanted. But things get even worse. Both of John's sons were getting divorced. This meant that whatever they received would be included in the divorce settlement, and they would probably lose half! From an estate originally worth £1,000,000, the four children would end up paying £300,000 in inheritance tax, and John's sons would lose half of what they inherited to divorce – John's sons expected inheritance of £250,000 each would become only £87,500!

Unfortunately this small example is not unusual. So often we find that Wills are written in isolation, do not take account of a person's family situation and are written without any thought to pending tax changes.

This is why we decided to write this book.

If you're reading this book you're one of two people. Either you're an academic estate and tax practitioner and using this to help you through your exams, or simply to give you more ideas about how to deal with the estate planning of your own clients. Alternatively, you are an individual looking to do some form of estate plan. What do we mean by estate plan?

An estate plan means organizing your personal and financial affairs in such a way that in the event of your death you have passed your assets to the people that you want to and at the time that you want them to inherit, without the wrong people inheriting. That's the purpose of an estate plan.

An estate plan is designed to make sure that it benefits the people who inherit, rather than cause or contribute to any problems. It should be put together not just as a vehicle to reduce tax, but also as a vehicle to enhance the lives of the beneficiaries, be it children, grandchildren, charities, or third parties. That's what a good estate plan does.

The purpose of this book is to explain the overriding principles of putting an estate plan together. We talk about importance of the Will and how that affects the structure of an estate plan. We talk about inheritance tax and what impact that could have on your estate, not just from a financial standpoint but from an emotional one too. Because inheritance tax is too big a subject and too changeable a subject to fully explain and dissect in a printed book, we have included the most popular techniques for mitigating inheritance tax legally, in ways the HMRC and the Treasury are perfectly happy to approve.

This book will also go through the practicalities of what happens upon death; what things you need to be thinking about prior to death so that you can organize your affairs, so that whoever deals with everything following your death can deal with it effectively with the minimum hassle and upset. When someone passes away, it's usually a family member who deals with most of the deceased's affairs, and it is usually a traumatic and emotional time. That is why the more you can do prior to your death, the easier and less disruptive their job will be. This part also covers the more emotional practicalities; what knowledge, stories, secrets and advice do you want to pass on to your family?

Finally, we'll talk about the characteristics of the people who actually put an estate plan together effectively. If you know you are a very particular, analytical, detail-orientated person, and there is even a slight chance that you'd find it hard to fully leave the planning of your estate in the hands of a professional, you might want to go straight to Part VI, before reading the rest of the book.

Read about the characteristics of somebody who plans their estate successfully and decide if that's you. If it's not, quite honestly, it's possible that reading on isn't the best idea for you. If you feel that you can develop the skills and the approach necessary to plan your estate well, or if you find that you already have the right characteristics, this book will help you decide exactly what you want to achieve, who's going to benefit, the impact inheritance tax will have on the people you leave behind, and all the practicalities to consider. Jump straight in and let us update your knowledge and guide you through all the preparations you can do before going to a professional to draw up your Will.

Whilst this book contains some technical information, it is written for the layman and woman, and we try to give real examples of real situations to highlight points along the way.

Of course we've changed names and figures to protect both the innocent and the guilty! Yet all of the examples and all of the stories in this book come from our practice.

We are an estate planning practice, and we have over 40 years of combined experience in dealing not just with setting up estate plans together with the investment plans that we put in place, but we also work closely with the families following the death of a client. This gives us more experience in how to put an estate plan together than many other companies in this space. The families are the people who are left to pick up the pieces when the time comes. It's from that experience that we've put this book together.

The book was put together because we wanted to share our thoughts on estate planning. Unfortunately, we cannot work with everybody. We can only deal with a certain number of people and generally, we'll deal with people who are geographically local. This book is designed to help those who aren't able to work with us directly and those who are working with other estate planners but want a wider view on what they could do, as much as it is written for our clients who wish to learn more about the estate planning process.

When putting the book together, we focussed on the readers and how the book can be used to generate effective solutions that can actually be implemented. We considered the reasons why these solutions and other processes may not be used or followed through on, and seek to address those reasons throughout.

Our aim for this book is to provide you with the definitive guide to successful estate planning, using easy to action content and formats. With that said, this book is not intended to be a buffet. We recommend you read it all, in order, even if you have some existing knowledge of the topics outlined.

Thank you very much for taking the time to read this book, and we thank you in advance for the decisions and actions you will take after reading. We want you to feel well-equipped and confident that you have everything you need to make informed financial and emotional decisions about your own future, and that of your family.

1

PART

Wills

Chapter 1
Introduction To Wills

Wills can often be confusing and stressful. If you've done a Will in the past or you've played a part in executing someone else's Will, then you may well have felt this way. We can assure you though, it's normal to feel like that if you haven't had the right guidance and support. Over the years of working with adults at all stages of life, one thing we've found is that most people know they should have a Will, but they don't fully understand why or what it involves. Furthermore, despite the fact that so many people don't know the answer to the question, "Why do I need a Will?" or more specifically, "Why do I need a Will now?", unfortunately very few actually ask.

Sometimes people feel embarrassed about admitting that they don't know because it makes them feel vulnerable, or they feel as though they've made a mistake and honestly if that's you, please don't worry. It's extremely common. So common in fact, we're going to look at what Wills really are, where they came from, and why it's important you have one before we go into further detail on anything else. If you think you do know why you need a Will, we would ask that you read this section anyway. Everything we discuss in this book hinges on the level of understanding contained in this chapter, so even if you don't learn anything completely new, it will at least refresh and update your existing knowledge.

1.1 What Is A Will?

Wills today are based on the Will Act of 1837. Prior to that they were more of a social matter, intended originally for men without an heir. Luckily for us, the Wills Act has been updated in the last couple of centuries but nonetheless, some of the practicalities of a Will are outdated and archaic. For example, some of the language is still written in Latin.

They can also be complex due to a combination of old laws and new laws, making them challenging for the untrained average adult to navigate. We're going to simplify and explain all of that for you in this book. The one thing that continues to remain relevant to us today, before we go into all of that, is a Will's purpose.

A Will is a legal document designed to give every adult, or testator, the right to distribute their assets as they see fit. The testator creates the Will, and entrusts the executor to action or implement it - the executor very often becomes a trustee who holds the assets in the Will before they are then transferred to the beneficiaries, who actually benefit from them.

Despite this being a good thing that can benefit all of us and with more help on offer than ever before, only two thirds of the UK currently have one. This is outrageous if you think about it. After the boom in homeownership created by the sale of council houses in the 1980s people in the UK are more wealthy than ever before, making the use of a Will even more important.

1.2 Why Have A Will?

Back in the late eighties, we arranged some loans for a couple who were probably in their mid-30s, and they had four children. One evening, they went to the cinema, leaving their parents to look after the kids. On the way back, they were both killed outright in a car crash. Suddenly the children, all aged between two and seven, were parentless. The police tracked down the grandparents, went over to the house, delivered this horrific news and then let them know that Social Services would be around shortly to take the children into care.

The grandparents were obviously heartbroken; not only had they lost one of their own children but now they were about to lose their young grandchildren and didn't even know where they'd be going or who'd be looking after them. They insisted the children stay with them but the police officer explained that the children were now wards of the court because neither of the parents had a Will.

Less than 24 hours after their parents were killed, the children were taken away from their grandparents and handed over to their local authority who would then decide who would look after them going forwards. There was no Will to state the parents' wishes for their children, so the authorities were automatically identified as the decision-makers. Not the grandparents.

The grandparents then had to make an application to the court to take parental responsibility for the children and legally become their guardians, which took three weeks. They were granted guardianship in the end, but not before those poor children had to spend three weeks in foster care having just lost both their parents.

This story has to highlight one of the strongest reasons to ever have a Will. There is simply no reason good enough to avoid it, when the situation above is a possible outcome. That is a real life example. If you have children and any form of meaningful asset, you need a Will. The alternatives are just not worth the risk.

If you have no Will, you are subject to intestacy. This is a big problem for individuals and families as the story above shows, but it's also a problem for society because if you pass away without a Will and no next of kin comes forwards or heir hunters can't track them down, all unclaimed inheritance will pass to the Duchy of Cornwall. There are millions of unclaimed pounds out there that are going straight into the government's pockets because people haven't written their final wishes out in a valid Will. The reasons this happens are varied.

Some don't want to think about dying and tell themselves they have plenty of time, whereas others have a Will then get divorced, get remarried or go through some other life change and either don't realise their previous Will is now invalid, they think it'll be too costly to update, or they bury their heads in the sand. Others get suspicious that if they write their Will they're somehow tempting fate and the inevitable will happen sooner than it otherwise would do.

Ultimately, we all know deep down these are not reasons. They're excuses. Understandable excuses of course; death is scary and unpleasant. But addressing these things now and getting your Will done properly will save you and your loved ones a lot of stress and heartache when the time comes. Here's an example of what we mean.

Imagine you drafted a Will at some point in the past, but it became invalid years ago and you didn't rewrite it, and then you pass away. You are close to your niece on your spouse's side. She's the person you rely on the most for companionship and care as you have no kids of your own and your spouse passed away a few years ago. As you fall ill, your niece looks after you the most out of all your family members. You give her power of attorney in the case of your incapacity but when you do die, all your assets automatically go to your next of kin. In this case, it's your brothers and sisters.

You didn't want that. You wanted to take care of your niece the way she deserved; just like she'd taken care of you. How would you feel if that happened? The number one reason people walk through our doors is that they want to make sure the right people get their assets, and certain others do not.

It's therefore important that you fully understand what you need to do to make sure your loved ones are protected, no matter how difficult it seems. The good news is with the right help, it doesn't have to be practically difficult. True professionals will alleviate those challenges for you and give you the facts you need to know.

1.3 Requirements Of A Will

There are several ways of creating a Will, certain people involved and indeed, certain requirements that must be met to make a Will valid.

Firstly, you could create your Will orally with a witness present. You can state verbally how you want your assets to be divided and where you want them to go. The witness is there to confirm your wishes after your death. While this is still a valid way of creating a Will today, it's not used because it's unreliable.

It was widely used back in the 1800s and early 1900s when people were less wealthy, the legal framework surrounding Wills was less robust and there was no advice available. The witness could be anyone, but it's a role that used to be performed mainly by priests. These days, it would be more likely to be a doctor or a loved one, but of course you're opening your family up to all kinds of difficulties if they've only got somebody's word for it.

Alternatively, you can simply write down what you'd like to happen to your assets in the event of your death. There are no legal guidelines on drafting a Will; no legal requirements for how it's written. The issue with that way is there are hundreds and hundreds of laws and methods governing how you choose to distribute your assets.

These vary depending on property, tax, trusts, who you want to inherit, gifts made during your lifetime, the date of your Will, your marital status...the list goes on. Unless you know the system, exactly what you want to happen and the most efficient way to achieve that, you want to write your Will with the guidance and support of a professional advisor. The costs are outweighed by the protection they offer.

If you remember the TV presenter and actress Lynda Bellingham, you probably know she died of cancer in 2014 and reportedly wanted everything to be distributed between her two sons[1]. However, her Will wasn't crystal clear and at the time of writing, it is still in dispute because, according to her sons, her third husband is trying to hold onto the money for himself.

They also claim he's squandered thousands of it already, and reportedly evicted them from their family home.[2] No-one likes to think that the people they love most in the world could fall out and fail to take care of each other in your absence, but sadly, where money's involved, it happens all the time.

1.3.1 You & Your Witnesses

The person who writes the Will is known as the testator. You have to be over 18 years old. You also have to be of sound mind. You must sign your Will and when you do, there must be exactly two witnesses present. Without two witnesses, the Will is invalid.

The purpose of the witnesses is to say that you are signing your Will under no undue pressure. For this reason, your

---

1 Source: http://www.dailymail.co.uk/news/article-3536017/Lynda-Bellingham-s-widower-hits-row-sons.html
2 Source: http://www.huffingtonpost.co.uk/entry/lynda-bellingham-widower-husband-michael-pattemore-sons-will-dispute-new-house_uk_571c8950e4b0727e4fe797c3

witnesses should be totally independent people. They are simply there to witness your signature. They're not witnessing the contents of the Will. All they're saying is that you're signing free of any duress or any undue influence, and also that this is your signature. They're not saying that they've read a copy of the Will or that they agree with any of the contents. If your witnesses have any qualms about your ability to sign your Will free of undue pressure or without presence of mind, they shouldn't act.

There is one more key rule. Your witnesses cannot be beneficiaries or executors. If someone witnesses a Will, any benefits assigned to them within the Will are null and void. It's the same if they are assigned as an executor. Their responsibilities to execute the Will will overtake any benefits the Will says they should receive.

We once worked with a gentleman who'd left his brother £50,000 in his Will but also asked him to witness it. We noticed and pointed out to him that if he wanted his brother to get that £50,000, he should redo his Will, getting someone else to witness it that time. It turned out he'd done it on purpose! He didn't want him to get the money and wanted him to find out after he was gone as an act of revenge for his brother stealing a girlfriend when they were in college!

1.3.2 Signing & Dating Your Will

Your Will must be signed and dated. While dating it is not a legal requirement, it is incredibly important. This is recommended for a number reasons, which we'll explore later in the book, but one reason it's particularly important to date your Will is that every Will states, "This is the last Will and testament of [name] and will supercede any other". In dating your Will every single time you do one, you are ensuring that it is the most valid version in the eyes of the law. A key point to note is that it's not the date the Will is created that's significant; it's the date the Will is signed.

If you simply say, "This is my last Will and testament on the 20th July 2016", that's just a statement. It doesn't actually form the Will, legally, until you sign it. Even though signing and dating your Will ensures the most recent version is valid, your Will is an ambulatory document until you die.

Circumstances can change. Whatever you draft is not legally binding because of the ambulatory nature of the Will. It only becomes enforceable in the instance of your death: if the laws at the time of your death have changed from the laws at the time you formed your Will, the new laws will take precedent. Each time new legislation comes in that affects your Will, the Will becomes less and less effective. Legislative changes effectively dilute your Will over time so in dating and signing your Will, you are simply stating your intentions at that time. Not at the time at which you die.

Since you only write a Will to state your intentions for when you die, a lot of people don't understand how the date could make it mean something else. Let's say you want to leave everything to your children, and in your Will you say, "to my children", and you date it. After that, you have another child. In the eyes of the law, your Will says it's only the children who existed before the date on your signed Will that are going to inherit anything. Instead you could say that you leave your estate to your children born now and in the future, so it goes past the date on your Will. You have to be careful that the date doesn't draw a line. Alternatively in some cases, you might want it to draw a line.

Dating and signing go hand in hand as they define the moment at which your intentions were decided upon. However there are some best practices to make sure it's done correctly. For dating, the date must be totally clear, with no crossings out and no amendments. If it's not signed correctly, it will be totally unenforceable. That was the problem with Lady Diana's Will. She actually died intestate because it wasn't signed correctly.

Now that we've looked at some of the requirements of a Will, we'll investigate what you can do to prepare for writing it.

Chapter 2
Preparing To Write Your Will

Imagine that you wanted to bake a cake for your dad who was ill. You start with the flour, eggs, a little milk and caster sugar, and begin mixing. After a couple of minutes you check the recipe only to discover that it needed salt! There's no salt in the house, all the salt cellars are empty, and now you have a big eggy mess. If only you had prepared and read the recipe before starting. As with all important things in life, preparation can be the difference between creating something amazing and creating a disaster! Now we've been through what a Will is and the basic requirements and recommendations for creating one, let's go through the people and things you need to consider and information you need to gather before drafting yours.

2.1 Know Your Estate

The first step in preparation for drafting your Will is knowing what's in your estate. This includes both your assets and your liabilities. It's a good idea to make a list of everything and keep it updated as you go. In our experience, people tend to know their tangible assets such as their house, ISA etc., and liabilities such as a mortgage and credit cards, but forget the items that are less visible on a day to day basis, such as their insurance policies. If you have life cover of £500,000, it should go in your Will.

People are often unsure of pensions. Pensions are not subject to Will conditions. There is a form called a Nomination Of Benefits form which is separate to your Will. If you've ever filled one of these out it would have been while in employment. It's easy to forget ever doing this, but they typically place your agreed pension into a Master Trust arrangement, along with any death benefits included, so your pension is an asset, but it's directed separately from your Will.

It's therefore important not to forget about updating your Nomination of Benefits form! Likewise with service benefits, you could direct the employer to leave them to your spouse after death, but if your spouse dies or you remarry, and you have not updated your instructions, then nobody would receive the money.

While not exhaustive, the following is a list of common assets:

- The home (residential)
- Investment property
- Savings in bank accounts
- Stocks and shares
- Other investment assets

- Interests in absolute or interest in possession trusts

- A business, or shares in businesses

- Vehicles

- Jewellery

- Chattels

- National Savings

- Life insurance

- Pension lump sums

- Income, interest or dividends received since death

Assets and Liabilities

Write out in the spaces below your assets and liabilities, making sure to include everything.

Assets

Your home	£_____
Other property	£_____
Your contents and cars	£_____
Your investments	£_____
Your pensions	£_____
Life insurance	£_____
Death in service	£_____
Other	£_____
Total	£_____

Liabilities

Mortgage	£_____
Loans	£_____
Other	£_____
Total	£_____

2.2 The Family Tree

It might sound obvious, but knowing who is in your family and therefore who is a potential beneficiary is important. We've found that drawing out your family tree is a great way to determine where everything might go, and that mapping everyone out in a visual format helps when considering "What happens if...". Having backup plans in case of a sudden change in circumstance is a very good idea.

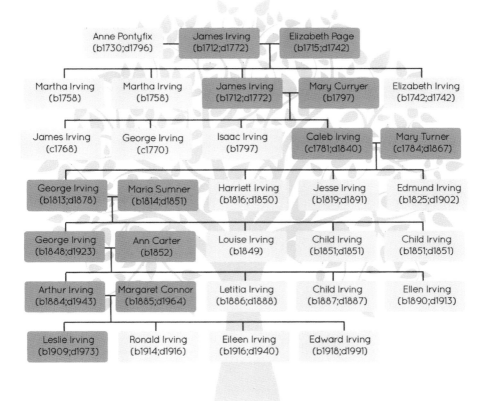

In our experience, clients often think they already know who they'll include in the Will, but things can get unexpectedly complicated. For example, with illegitimate children. You have to consider not only what you want, but also your moral obligations. Anyone in your family, blood relative or not, should go on the family tree.

Then only after you've drawn it out in full should you make decisions on who to include as a beneficiary and who to exclude. This is in fact important from a legal standpoint, because if you're not clear on this, people who feel they should be included but aren't could try to make a claim on the estate in court. You could also make a separate list of non-family members who you'd like to benefit, but this is of course less important from a legal point of view.

EXERCISE

Draw Your Family Tree

As straightforward as it sounds: find a sheet of A4 paper and draw out your family tree. This will help you to visualise everyone in your family, note what their relation is to you, and so decide how best to distribute your assets, as well as show that you have considered whether to include or exclude every interested party.

2.3 What Do You Want, And Not Want?

Having drawn out your family tree and considered who could lay a claim on the estate, you must now think carefully about exactly what you want the Will to accomplish. You must also ensure that, when it's written, it reflects your wishes accurately.

For example, if your partner has children from a previous relationship whom you'd like to include in the Will, you have to be specific. Rather than saying "The children", say "The children of my spouse".

We once worked with a couple, Mr and Mrs Smith,[3] who left everything to each other in their Wills. In the event of the second death, everything was to go to their son. They meant the man they'd raised as their son, Bob, but hadn't specified that Bob was not Mr Smith's biological son. Legally, they'd failed Bob because they hadn't specified who they meant and their solicitor hadn't asked the nature of the relationship. Luckily we spotted it, but this could have left Bob with nothing. It's a different situation with adoption; because the child is legally the couple's, it doesn't need to be stated that they are not biologically related.

Be sure that your language is crystal clear with no room for doubt as to who the beneficiary should be, and if you have professional help be sure to let them know the full picture, so that your wishes can be carried out correctly after death.

---

3 All names throughout the book have been changed to protect the identity of those involved.

2.4 Consider Gifts

So we've now worked out the extent of your estate, the interested parties in your family have begun to think about your wishes; the next thing to consider is exactly what to gift. There are three main types of gift that can be given in a Will - objects, fixed sums of cash, and percentages of the estate. We'll talk in much more detail about gifting in Section 3.3, but begin thinking now about who should get what, and when.

The question of when to gift is a very common concern i.e. On death? On the second death? Another event? We frequently find that people die too wealthy. They overestimate the amount of money they'll need in their older years, and as a result, there's more for their families to sort out and more tax to pay.

You must also take account of gifts made during your lifetime. For example, if you have three children and gave your eldest daughter £20,000 towards a deposit on a house and then die unexpectedly, and your Will indicated that everything was meant to be divided equally between all three children, then the eldest would have £20,000 more than the other two because of the gift. Therefore, you should consider if the Will should have some form of gift equalization included, and if so, how should this work.

The Will is actually one of the weakest documents to pass on assets as a gift. In the future, circumstances and legislation can change and a poorly written Will can end up mired in legal proceedings. It's much more secure and reliable to set up trusts during your lifetime. We would therefore suggest that you try to work out exactly how much money you will need for the rest of your life, then gift the rest before it comes to passing it on in the Will. We would also suggest that your Will be as clear and up to date as possible, so that any gifts you do give can be executed smoothly.

2.5 Who Should Draft The Will?

The final step of preparation for you to consider is who you'd like to draft the Will. Technically you can draft your Will and allocate gifts yourself; there's no legal format and you can get the necessary forms from the Post Office.

However, by doing this you are opening yourself up to all sorts of errors and problems. There are many complex laws surrounding Wills and trusts, and it's impossible to know what you don't know. It's important, therefore, that you use a specialist; someone who is 'STEP qualified'. They can be difficult to find, so you'll need to do some research. While a solicitor may be qualified to draft your Will, are they a specialist?

A specialist will not only be on the ball with recent legislation and precedent changes but will also have a deep understanding of all the tax implications when drafting a Will. This is one of the biggest errors that we see; too many are written without consideration of taxation. The introduction of the Residential Nil Rate Band in April 2017, phased through to 2020, means that only someone who understands the details of these rules should draft your Will.

STEP stands for the 'Society of Tax and Estate Planning

Practitioners'. They are effectively the specialist professional body for estate planning. There is also a separate 'Will Society', and being a member of this is useful, but there are many more requirements and qualifications needed to become a member of STEP.

Standard things a STEP qualified specialist can help you with include working out how to efficiently deal with tax implications, ensuring all necessary information is included in the Will to avoid contestations and, if you have children, setting up an education and maintenance clause whereby the gifts for the children are held in a trust until they are 18 years old.

Chapter 3

Structuring Your Will

Now that you've made preparations to begin writing your Will, made a tally of your assets and liabilities and thought about your wishes, we're ready to look at how a Will is actually structured. There are a lot of different elements to consider and decisions to be made, so let's jump in!

3.1 Who Is Involved In The Will

The roles of the testator (yourself) and the witnesses have already been described in detail in Chapter 1, but there are several other key people involved in the Will.

3.1.1 The Executor

Executors are the people who are going to actually implement the Will. A lot of careful thinking needs to be put into choosing your executor. Many people will simply choose, for example, a family member or a solicitor without considering the ramifications of this choice.

The main reason this choice is so important is that 90% of

Wills (and all good Wills) create a dispersal trust on death. This is different from a normal trust, in that it is simply an administrational tool to collect all the money and assets from the estate together before it is passed on.

Significantly, the executor is entirely in charge of this dispersal trust: they are the trustee. If the Will instructs that "all my estate should go to my daughter Sally", the executor would be in charge of all that money until it reaches Sally. There is little to no oversight of the executor, as we discuss in the next section, so it's important to ensure they are someone you trust implicitly. We would like to think that after our death our chosen executor, perhaps a close friend or family member, would not run off with the money, but this does happen.

Note: Trusts In The Will

Although most Wills create a dispersal trust, we would generally advise against creating a regular trust within the Will. These are subject to the circumstances, legislation and precedent at the time of death. It can therefore be dangerous to have a Will create them, as you cannot know what those circumstances will be. There are some instances where this may be acceptable, but by and large if you want to set up a trust then set it up yourself in your lifetime, rather than letting a Will do so.

We'll now go into more detail on choosing your executor, and then go over some of the costs that can be associated with hiring a bank or solicitor to execute the Will.

3.1.1.1 Choosing Your Executor

There are two main issues to consider here: the capacity of the executor in the future, and the level of responsibility they hold.

Often choosing someone of your own age as an executor is a bad idea, as generally we will die when we're old, gently we hope, and so they too will be old. Will they have the capacity to carry out the job as needed?

Let's think about this further. Say that you wanted to distribute half your money to your young grandson, Jack, aged three. He can only inherit if both the Will instructs that he should and if legislation says that he can. Unfortunately, you have to have the age of majority before you can inherit, i.e. be 18 years of age. Once probate is granted, the executor would distribute the other half of the money as instructed by the Will, and would be the trustee of all Jack's inheritance for 15 years. You should ask yourself not only whether your chosen executor would be able to execute the Will soon after your death, but whether - if required - they could continue doing so for years to come.

This brings us back to the issue of trusts raised earlier. If you add up everything you have and estimate you are worth 1, 2, 3 million etc., ask yourself, "Do I trust this executor to hold onto that money for 1 year, 5 years, 15 years?" This is especially important if you're leaving money to grandchildren, as in the example of Jack above.

Additionally, the executor (who becomes the trustee) is not really checked by anybody, which is why - more often than we'd like to think - they can run off with the estate. It's possible that there could be some form of random check by the court but that's incredibly unlikely, and the probate officer's primary job is to ensure there are no issues with the Will itself and that the correct tax is paid, so it's entirely up to the beneficiaries, or any interested party, to either challenge the Will or challenge the work that the executor is doing. It's a very important position, so choose wisely.

3.1.1.2 Costs And Professionals

There is the option to have a professional executor distribute the assets, and this can either be a bank or a solicitor. Although these are regulated, in almost every case the fees for executing a Will are unlimited; they charge a flat percentage of the estate, no matter how straightforward a Will it might be.

> **"** "I saw this in action first-hand with my Nan and Grandad's estate when I was still in school. A bank was named as the executor in the Will, and when my Grandad passed away, Nan paid 3% of the estate to them. Then when Nan passed away they charged another 3%, so they effectively received 6%, reducing the worth of the estate by a noticeable amount."
>
> **David**

The size of the estate doesn't denote its complexity; a large estate might be very simple to execute, just as a small estate might be very complicated. Nonetheless, the size of the estate will often dictate how much solicitors and banks will charge. In fact, this is where the term 'goodwill' comes from. The way that solicitors practices used to be valued was based on the number of Wills that they held in the vault (the number of 'good Wills' that they had) because they could rely on them as future income. If you are the executor of someone's estate, when that person dies you know you're going to make money from it, so the more Wills that you had in storage on which you were an executor, the more valuable your practice, and hence the term goodwill.

As a general rule of thumb, then, we'd advise against a bank being an executor unless you have an incredibly complex set of circumstances, such as passing on foreign property through the Will, described in the box below, and there's nobody that you can trust, and nobody that can do the job. Otherwise there's no real reason to pay a professional.

Note: Foreign Property And Inheritance Tax

Inheritance tax must be always be paid before probate can be approved and the assets distributed. In cases with foreign property inheritance this can become a real annoyance, as you have to prove probate in the countries where the assets are held. You then have to do cross-referencing inheritance tax calculations, and you may in fact have to pay inheritance tax twice, once at home and once abroad.

Proving probate would be dependent upon the testamentary rules of the country where the property is held; it's not based on UK law. Under a recent EU directive, U.K. Wills can be used in other member countries, however who knows what will happen with Brexit as a separate treaty will now need to be made with all other 27 EU countries.

As an example, many Brits own property in Spain. In addition to various differences in inheritance law between our two countries which adds complexity, there is also no inheritance tax treaty between the British and Spanish. This means that any inheritance tax you pay in Spain (and you would have to pay it) would not be deducted from the tax you pay here, so you pay twice.

Essentially if you have property outside the UK then you will definitely want to consider using a professional executor / trustee. Or, even better, give the property away before this becomes an issue! Passing foreign property down through a Will is not recommended at all.

Another general rule of thumb is that we would always recommend against naming a solicitor or administrator as the executor in the Will. It's much better to have a layperson execute the Will who can hire professional assistance if needed. This is because after death - or if you were to suddenly lose capacity as you grow older - your Will, and hence the executor, can no longer be changed. Only the testator, alive and with full capacity, can change the executor.

This might lead to a situation where you've appointed a solicitor as executor, and after your death your children decide they don't want the solicitor to be involved; they want to execute the Will themselves. Unfortunately the solicitor is perfectly entitled to say, "Tough. I'm the executor, you've got to work with me". A professional executor can resign from the job but they can't be removed against their will.

On the other hand, if you named a layperson - for example your daughter - as executor and she was not able to do the job, she would be free to hire a solicitor to help out, and would also be free to fire that solicitor if she was unhappy with their work. She would also be able to agree the charges herself, which would not be possible had the solicitor been named in the Will directly.

To sum up: only if the Will is very complex and there is nobody that you can trust enough, and nobody that can do the job, would you name a bank as the executor. In every other circumstance it's usually best to name a trusted layperson, who can hire and fire professionals of their choice to help out as needed.

3.1.2 Guardians

If you have any children under the age of 18 then it is very important to name a guardian for them in your Will. Some people assume that a child's godparents become legal guardians after death, but this is not the case. Godparents have a religious and moral role, not a legal one. Without clear instructions, parental responsibility can pass to the government rather than to what might seem a logical family member, and the child may be taken into foster care until a court can decide where to send them.

There was a case in Wales a few years ago of an unmarried father whose partner died during childbirth; because he was not married to the mother, and there were no instructions in the Will, the baby was not legally his responsibility on her death. The court fast-tracked a decision and to his great relief it granted him parental responsibility, but the baby was taken away from him for a week before this nonetheless[4]. These are not situations we'd want our loved ones to have to deal with immediately after our death.

---

4 For more information on legal parental responsibility see: http://childlawadvice.org.uk/information-pages/parental-responsibility/

When choosing a guardian there are several main factors to consider. First of all, just like the executor, the guardian may need to carry out their duties for years to come after the event of your death.

Appointing your parents as guardians might seem like a fine idea when the child is a baby, but they will be responsible for the child until he or she turns 18. How old might your parents be by then? Would they still be the best choice? A common mistake people make is to appoint a guardian out of a sense of obligation. "If I don't appoint my mum she's going to be really upset," or something similar. This happens a lot, but the most important thing is not appeasing the feelings of family members, it's the wellbeing of the child.

Secondly, it's important to remember that the guardian is responsible for the emotional well being of the child; they're not responsible for the finances. In other words, they're not expected to use their own money to bring up the child: the assets within the estate would be used by the guardians for this purpose. For example, let's say a Mr Smith died and his children go to his brother to bring them up; he might need to buy a new house because he suddenly needs four bedrooms instead of two. The cost of that could be taken from the estate as it's a genuine expense.

Another common mistake when considering potential guardians is to look at their financial situation and conclude that they couldn't afford to look after your children. This should never be a consideration, because, as stated above, they will not be expected to use their own money anyway. Even if the estate itself is relatively small, remember that any life insurance policy ought to be enough to cover the cost of raising children. Of course this does mean that the estate may have eroded somewhat by the time the children reach maturity, but the guardian would nevertheless not be expected to use their own money.

Thirdly, remember that your decision could have a large impact on the child's life. If the child were still only a baby, it doesn't really matter whereabouts in the world the guardian lives; on your death the baby could go to live on the other side of the country with a relative and not realise what happened. But if the child is, say, a young teenager, with a school and a group of friends in the local area, you have to consider if the best move would still be to send them to live with a guardian far away, to uproot them entirely from their life immediately after the death of their parents.

Or would it be better to update the Will so that the guardian, rather than a geographically distant relative, is a local family friend (assuming they are willing and able to do it)?

As we've already stated, don't let a sense of obligation make the decision for you. A close family member is not inherently the best choice. You are the best judge of the loved ones around you, so consider your relationships with both family and friends, and take into account how moving to live with the chosen guardian would affect the life of the child. Let that help shape your decision.

Who Would You Choose As A Guardian

After considering the above points, use a blank sheet of paper or the space below to make a list of potential guardians who would make the most sense at different times in your child's life.

_____

_____

_____

_____

_____

_____

_____

_____

_____

_____

_____

_____

_____

_____

_____

_____

_____

_____

Remember that the Will is a living, breathing document, it can and should be updated regularly as circumstances change, in both your life and other people's lives, and that this is especially important when it comes to appointing the most suitable guardian for your children.

3.1.3 Beneficiaries

Beneficiaries are the named recipients of assets from the estate in the Will. They are the people you'd like to leave your worldly possessions to after death. We'll go into more detail regarding gifting to beneficiaries of the Will in the next few sections, but two important points to note, mentioned previously, is that beneficiaries cannot be a witness to the signing of the Will, and they cannot legally inherit until the age of majority.

3.2 Expressing Your Wishes

Now that we understand the roles of everyone involved we come to the actual content of the Will itself: expressing how you'd like your assets to be distributed after death. For clients this is often the most important part of the process of creating a Will: working out how best to pass on your estate. There are, naturally, many things to consider when choosing exactly how to do this, which we'll dig into now.

3.2.1 Specific Gifts

Specific gifts are named, concrete amounts or items to be gifted to individuals by the Will (as opposed to dividing up the residual estate - see Section 3.3.3). There are some pitfalls and tricks to ensuring that everything is fair and goes ahead exactly as you intended.

3.2.1.1 Pecuniary Legacies

Pecuniary legacies are the most straightforward gift. They are a simple instruction in the Will to give a cash sum to an individual. The important thing to understand is that cash gifts come out of the estate before anything else is disbursed. For example, let's say in your Will you leave £50,000 to your brother, John, and the rest to your son, Sam: John would get his £50,000 before Sam gets the remainder of the estate. That means Sam's inheritance falls by £50,000.

It's also common to include a line in the Will for certain gifts to exclude them from inheritance tax. This doesn't mean that inheritance tax isn't paid at all, it just means that the named gift itself does not attract tax because inheritance tax is paid on the entire estate.

This means that the other beneficiaries end up paying proportionately more tax to make up the difference.

Going back to the example above, if you were to state that John's £50,000 should be free from inheritance tax, then the roughly £20,000 worth of inheritance tax that should have been paid on his gift will instead come out of Sam's share.

Having said all that, we generally would advise against naming fixed cash amounts in the Will, for two main reasons. Firstly, fixed amounts lose value over time as inflation rises (in twenty years the generous gift in your Will of £50,000 may seem much less generous!). Secondly, as pecuniary legacies take priority over the distribution of the residuary estate (i.e. the remaining estate to be divided up as a percentage - see Section 3.3.3), you can end up with a very unfair Will, especially if the estate has been eroded due to unforeseen circumstances.

Say at the time of writing the Will your estate was worth £350,000, and you specified your brother John to receive a £50,000 fixed cash sum, with the rest of the estate to go to your son Sam; then, due to the cost of private care later in life, the estate's worth is reduced to £75,000. John still receives his £50,000, but Sam's share of the estate is drastically reduced from £300,000 to £25,000. We would therefore recommend, to avoid such situations, sharing out the entire estate in percentages of its total worth.

3.2.1.2 Physical Gifts

As well as cash gifts there are the actual, physical things you own. There is no legal reason why you couldn't list every object in your possession in the Will directing exactly where you want them to go, however we recommend against listing too many items as it will make the Will far too long and complex. We had a client a few years ago who had listed over 100 items in the Will!

There are two main things to consider when deciding what to gift. Firstly, is the gift identifiable, will the executor be able to find it, and would the beneficiary want it? If the executor cannot identify or find the named gift this could cause serious issues were anyone to contest the Will, and if the beneficiary doesn't want it they may be left feeling confused as to why it was specifically passed on to them. Secondly, most things that are listed will have to be valued for probate purposes; an expensive gift of, say, a car or a pair of diamond earrings will need to be included in the value of the estate for tax purposes.

Essentially try to keep the list of gifts as simple as possible. The fewer items named the easier it will be to create and execute your Will.

3.2.1.3 Equalisation

As previously mentioned, when writing your Will you may very well want to divide your estate equally between a number of beneficiaries. Let's say you have two children, Sally and Brian, and in the Will you clearly instruct the estate to be divided 50/50 between the two of them.

However, Sally brings up the point that you gave Brian a gift of £30,000 on leaving home to get started. Sally, on the other hand, still lives at home and so has not yet received this gift. If you were to die suddenly, the Will would not take this lifetime gift into consideration, and Sally would essentially be left £30,000 worse off than Brian. This is a very common situation with parents who have a child of house-buying age and another younger child.

An equalisation clause can solve the problem. This clause in a Will takes into account any gifts that were made in your lifetime, so that everything is made equal by the Will. Of course, working out all gifts that were given in a lifetime can become very complex (adjusting for inflation etc.), so, returning to the example above, it would be have been best to give simultaneous and equal gifts to both Sally and Brian of £30,000 (if possible). A good way of doing this would be to set up a trust for both children at the same time so that technically the gift has already been given to both equally, even if the money is to be released to them from the trust at different times.

3.2.1.4 Letter Of Wishes

A letter of wishes is a useful tool to guide the executor without legally binding them to a course of action. For example, you could write that, should one of your beneficiaries not want a certain gift, that gift could instead go to a second named person.

One of the most common uses for a letter of wishes is to have the Will itself pass your entire estate to your spouse (as this is tax free), and then to write the executor a letter of wishes directing the spouse on how you'd like them to distribute the goods as gifts outside of the Will. This avoids inheritance tax while allowing you to pass on your estate as you intended; of course, as the letter of wishes is not legally binding the spouse has no obligation to actually fulfil the wishes written there, so you should be aware of that.

It is important to remember that a letter of wishes is exactly that...a letter of your wishes, and as such has no legal standing. Of course, a court will take the contents into account if they are ruling on the Will, but that is as far as it goes. When using a letter of wishes it is vitally important to NOT attach the letter of wishes to the Will, as this may invalidate the Will. Ensure that it is kept with the Will, but is not attached to it in any way.

3.2.2 Gifts To Charities

Many people choose to leave money to charities, and there are good reasons for doing so. Not only do charitable donations avoid inheritance tax, they can also mean that you'll pay less inheritance tax on the remainder of the estate. If you were to donate 10% or more of the net value of your estate (after allowances such as the Nil Rate Band have been deducted) to charity in the Will, then the inheritance tax on the remaining 90% of the estate would be reduced from 40% to 36%.[5]

If this is something you intend to do, always remember to put the charitable reference number in the Will so that the correct charity can be identified, as their names often change with time. If the charity no longer exists, there is an element of UK law called the cy-près doctrine which allows the executor to pass the gift on to a charity of a similar nature. Also remember that the term 'charity' covers a wide range of organisations, from private schools to academic membership societies to environmental awareness organisations.

There are two ways to leave money to a charity, either as a fixed amount (say £500) or as a percentage of the estate (say 2%). If you leave a percentage of your estate to a charity, they will require you to undertake a full valuation of the estate

---

5 Note that gifts to charities during your lifetime, while they do fall outside your estate, have no effect on the rate of inheritance tax due after your death - so remember to gift to charity in the Will, rather than during your lifetime!

before you can release money to them. In our experience every charity will want to check and review the full set of valuations that you've done to make sure they're getting their fair share, adding a good deal of time and complexity to the process. Unlike with individual gifts, then, our general advice is to give specific legacies rather than a percentage of the estate to charity.

3.3.3 Residual Estate

The residual estate is everything that is to be divided up once all specific gifts have been given. If you wanted to share your estate out between your four children equally, they would each receive 25% in the Will, minus any gifts you have previously specified. As already detailed in Section 3.3.1, it is usually best to divide as much of your assets as possible as part of the residual estate to avoid any unintentional unfairness.

Remember that fixed gifts will always come out the Will first, and in the event that the estate has eroded due to unforeseen circumstances, giving a fixed sum of money to one beneficiary could leave your other loved ones with much less in the residual estate than you had planned.

Chapter 4

Changing Your Will

We've emphasised already that the Will is a living, breathing document which should be continually updated to be relevant to your circumstances as you grow older. This chapter will describe exactly how you can go about updating it, and contains some stories which may well convince you that keeping your Will up to date is a very good idea! There are four main ways that a Will can be changed: a codicil, a full rewrite, a deed of variation, and via legal situations.

4.1 Codicil

A codicil is an extra page added to a Will to change something within it. For example you might like to specify that Clause 5 of the Will, which gifted your canoe to Bill, now instead gifts it to Fred. By and large codicils are a bad idea, and we do not recommend using them, because they are easily messed up, changed, or lost.

There was a case once, Midland Bank vs. IRC, where Midland Bank as the executors of the Will submitted it to the probate office for approval. A third party then claimed the testator had written a codicil leaving money to him, and subsequently another third party appeared stating the same thing.

Although there was no codicil present, on the Will there was an impression of a paperclip, so it was held that the Will was unsafe because a codicil might have been attached originally and then removed. The probate office had to throw the Will out and declare the estate intestate. It's very important to never attach anything you don't intend to be a part of the Will.

There are no specific rules governing the format of codicils, it must simply be something the probate office will accept; the standard wording that is generally used is not strict. Technically it could be a handwritten note from the testator changing the entire spirit of the Will, but as we have already stated, codicils almost inevitably go wrong. Unless you are making a very straightforward change of information such as an address, we would recommend avoiding codicils altogether and instead rewrite the Will.

4.2 Rewrite

The second option, to entirely rewrite the Will, is almost always what we recommend. If you wish to make any meaningful change at all there is much less room for error by replacing the whole thing than, for example, by adding a codicil, as we have seen. It's absolutely vital when rewriting to include a revocation clause, which revokes and invalidates all previous Wills, and it's vital that the date on the new Will is more recent than that of the previous Will. If the date was incorrect and your previous Will appeared to have been written later, then the revocation clause in your rewrite would not apply to it.

It is entirely possible to get into some very messy situations with multiple Wills; without a revocation clause in the rewrite, legally you have shown an intention that the two Wills are supposed to run alongside each other. There is absolutely no good reason to have more than one Will, so avoid at all costs! For example, if you wrote a Will which left everything to your husband, James, except for £50,000 to go to your sister, Celia, and then you rewrite your Will (forgetting to include a revocation clause) leaving everything to James and giving nothing to Celia, the £50,000 gift in the first Will could still be enforced because it was not revoked.

4.3 Deed Of Variation

A deed of variation is where a Will is varied following death. The only people who can vary it are the beneficiaries. It has to be approved by those beneficiaries who would lose out to the change. For example, if you were to leave your entire estate to your sister, and she declares that she doesn't want any of it, a deed of variation would be drawn up so that the estate could pass to someone else.

This happens fairly often, 10–20% of the time, often for legal or tax reasons. Although inheritance tax is paid on the estate after the deed of variation comes into effect, sharing out the estate in certain ways could save on tax in the long run (as long as it's approved by HMRC), usually in the event of the second death. Your Will might, say, leave everything to your child, putting them over the inheritance tax threshold in the event of their own death, so they could arrange a deed of variation to give some of the estate to your grandchildren.

In the run-up to the 2015 election you may remember it was reported that Ed Miliband's family had used a deed of variation to share out the estate between the two sons and their mother in such a way that, eventually, they would save on inheritance tax.[6] He received a lot of media attention and criticism for this (especially given his proposed changes to inheritance tax), although his family's use of the deed of variation was legitimate.

It's important to note, however, that a deed of variation cannot be used to evade inheritance tax: in the case Lau v HMRC (2009) STC (SCD) 352 it was deemed that the beneficiary had renounced their claim on the estate specifically in order that the asset could pass to a non-taxable beneficiary, who subsequently gifted the asset back to the first beneficiary, effectively evading the tax.[7]

Following this decision the balance between acceptable and unacceptable has greyed somewhat, but the main point to remember is that you shouldn't rely on a deed of variation to ensure your wishes are carried out. Legislation is changed often, and there is no guarantee that a variation will be permitted in the future when you die. It's best to include exactly how you'd like to distribute your assets within the Will itself; then if your

---

6 See for example this story in the Telegraph: www.telegraph.co.uk/finance/personalfinance/tax/11434504/Ed-Miliband-rewrote-his-fathers-will-to-cut-IHT.-Should-you-do-the-same.html
7 Lau vs HMRC (2009) www.withersworldwide.com/events/2009/margaret-lau-v-her-majestys-revenue-customs-com

beneficiaries decide (and are able) to vary the Will that is up to them.

4.4 Legal Situations

There are several legal situations where a Will can be challenged. A court may intervene because it decides the Will is unfair (although only for specific reasons that are often very difficult to prove, such as whether undue influence was exerted over the testator); because it appears the Will is a fraud; or because it believes the intentions of the testator were not reflected accurately by the Will (perhaps because it was written in old age and so a key heir was forgotten, or because it was changed in the last few months of life during a degenerative mental illness).

Challenging a Will in court is very expensive, and the executor of the Will that is challenged takes the money for their legal bills directly out of the estate, reducing the assets remaining for heirs. A challenge also delays the distribution of assets until the court has made a decision. Beneficiaries of the Will are therefore generally going to be unhappy with anyone who brings a challenge to court.

We'll now look at the legal ramifications of both marriage and divorce in relation to your Will.

4.4.1 Marriage

When you get married, any Will you have previously written becomes invalid, and you must create a new one. In the case of intestacy, your spouse receives all your personal property and belongings, the first £250,000 of the estate, and half of the remaining estate if there are any children, grandchildren or great-grandchildren to inherit the other half.

Many of our clients choose to write similar clauses into their Will, although we have encountered situations where this is not quite the case. There was a story a few years ago in one of the legal papers of a long distance truck driver who had died; when his estate was being divided, it became apparent that he had two separate families on opposite sides of the country.

He would spend the first half of the week with one family, and the second half with the other - neither wife had any idea. It came to light that both families had two children and a dog, that in both families all three had the same names, and that he wanted his estate to be divided equally between the two wives. Perhaps something to bear in mind when deciding what to gift your spouse!

4.4.2 Divorce

Unlike with marriage, divorce does not invalidate your previous Will. It only invalidates the sections relating to your spouse so they are no longer a beneficiary. It's not compulsory to update the entire document, but to keep everything crystal clear we would recommend that you do. You will also need to remember to update all documents outside of the Will, especially things like a Nomination of Benefits form.

There was a case around 12 years ago of a man, Ben, who

married his first wife, Janice, got divorced, and subsequently got married a second time to Emily. Ben's Will was updated both times he got married and once after the divorce, so that was all in order. However, his form directing death and service benefits and his company pension payout simply stated that "Everything should go to my wife".

Ben's second wife Emily went to collect the benefits, but she was officially challenged by Janice, as the form had been written, signed and dated while he was still married to Janice and had not been updated since then. The trustees decided that they would not pay anyone until the courts had sorted out who should get the money. That was 12 years ago, the money has still not been paid out, and the estate will have been reduced significantly by legal fees.

People often go to great lengths for money, especially after death when your feelings can no longer be hurt, so be sure to not leave any loopholes like Ben and keep all your documentation up to date.

PART

Inheritance Tax

Chapter 5

Introduction To Inheritance Tax

By now you'll have a reasonably good idea of why you need a Will, and what should be included in that Will. Next we get down to the nitty-gritty detail of inheritance tax. In this chapter you'll learn how inheritance tax is calculated, that tax avoidance and tax evasion are two very different things, and that taking every measure allowed within the law to avoid inheritance tax is perfectly acceptable and could save your beneficiaries a significant amount of money.

We should note here that all information provided was correct at the time of printing, but tax laws are complex, ever-changing entities. We also note that it would be impossible to cover every possible inheritance tax situation in this book; the information provided here will apply to most, but not all, people. We therefore strongly advise you to seek out a STEP qualified professional who can give you the most up-to-date facts and figures available for your exact set of circumstances

Note: Advice Seminars

For over 15 years, Wills & Trusts have been running

public education seminars explaining up-to-date and relevant techniques with regards to inheritance tax. If you wish to attend one of these seminars simply go to our website and you can book on for free.[8] There are no salesmen at these seminars and no products being pushed, they are purely educational.

5.1 Should I Avoid Inheritance Tax?

When people hear the term 'tax avoidance' they often assume it involves dodgy under-the-table deals to beat the taxman. This is because 'avoidance' is commonly confused with 'evasion', but they are not the same thing at all. Tax avoidance is perfectly legal, while evasion is entirely illegal.

For example, if you have an ISA, then you are not paying any income tax or any capital gains tax on the money in that account. Likewise, if you put money into a pension, you get the benefits of tax relief. Both of these are classed as tax avoidance. From the revenue's perspective, they consider inheritance tax as an optional tax liability, i.e. there are legitimate ways in which you can avoid paying the inheritance tax, provided you fit within the rules and you follow HMRC guidelines.

So, should you avoid it? A story which we often tell at this point is about one of our client's parents. His mum and dad inherited

---

8 See: www.wills-and-trusts.co.uk/seminars/

nothing in their life; his dad worked as a builder on sites, trying to build up his own estate. They didn't own a house, but rented, and they invested all their money into a building society, saving money to buy their first house. Soon after this the building society went bust and they lost all of their savings - every last penny - so they borrowed the deposit money from their uncle, and bought their very first house. Nobody else in the family had owned a house before, everybody else had lived in council housing. Then like most people in the 60s, 70s and 80s, they traded up, traded up, traded up, gradually living in more and more expensive houses, until now when they live in a property worth around £600,000, and have built up other financial assets which amount to perhaps £300,000. They made all that from nothing.

Their view is that over the course of their lifetime, they have paid income tax on every penny earned, VAT on every purchase made, stamp duty on every new house they bought. So they regard the money they have now as after-tax money; they built up a good-sized estate from nothing and paid their fair share along the way. For them, inheritance tax is extremely unfair - why should they pay tax on their estate, which has already been taxed, simply for wanting to pass it on to their children or grandchildren? They could have spent the lot so that neither the children, grandchildren nor taxman saw any of it, but of course this is not what they wanted to do. Their view, then, is that they should do everything they can, as long as it's legal, to reduce and mitigate inheritance tax.

Of course, there are some morally grey areas between

avoidance and evasion. You'll probably have read in the news early in 2016 about the 'Panama Papers' leak of 11.5 million documents from Panamanian law firm Mossack Fonseca. The scandal in the media revolved mostly around the revelation that David Cameron's father had an offshore fund in a tax haven, paying no tax in Britain.[8]

Although it could be argued that this was morally reprehensible, it was not illegal. On the other hand, some of the Mossack Fonseca shell corporations whose details were released in the leak were most certainly used for illegal purposes, including tax evasion. Their activities were different, but not vastly so, from the legal activities of the rest.

As avoidance creeps closer to evasion, then, you'll have to consult your own moral compass to decide how far to go, but to be clear, in this book we will only outline strategies for avoidance. Everything we discuss is totally accepted by HMRC, and is totally accepted by the inheritance tax office, with many precedents to show that there's no reason why these strategies shouldn't be used.

Now, hopefully with a slightly different perspective on how much inheritance tax you should be paying, let's look at how it's actually calculated.

5.2 How It's Calculated

The most straightforward explanation for calculating

---

8 See for example this story from the Guardian: http://www.theguardian.com/news/2016/apr/04/panama-papers-david-cameron-father-tax-bahamas

inheritance tax, in its current form, is that - for all UK domiciled individuals - the rate of tax is 40% paid on the net value of the estate excluding the first £325,000, which is tax-free. This tax-free allowance is known as the nil rate band. Spouses and civil partners may also exchange assets and leave them to each other in their Will without incurring any liability.

Of course, the above outline does not cover many of the more complicated details, which we'll look at now.

5.2.1 Nil Rate Band Explained

Every UK domiciled individual is entitled to the nil rate band (NRB), a tax-free allowance that can be passed on to beneficiaries without any liability. The present level of the NRB is £325,000. In 2007 new legislation introduced carry forward, a concept where, if you are married or in a civil partnership, and if you gift your estate to your spouse, they will benefit from your unused NRB. Specifically, the percentage of your NRB that was unused (due to the spouse or civil partner exemption) will transfer to them as a percentage of the current nil rate band at second death.

For example, if you were to leave 100% of your estate to your husband, then 100% of the allowance would be carried forward on your death. Then, should the NRB in the future increase from £325,000 to say £400,000, your husband, on their death, would have both yours and their own NRBs combined as tax free. In this case that would be his £400,000 plus 100% of the new NRB (also £400,000) = £800,000.

As another example, let's say that Liz and Janet are in a civil partnership. Liz makes a gift of £32,500 to her child, which effectively 'uses up' 10% of her NRB; she leaves the rest for Janet, so 90% of her NRB is carried forward. This means that, on the second death, Janet's NRB will be the new rate of £400,000, plus 90% of Liz's NRB (at the same new threshold), which is £360,000 = £760,000. If Liz's total estate was worth £800,000, then £40,000 would be liable for tax.

As you can see, deciding whether to gift to anyone other than your spouse / civil partner on the first death can make a big difference to the NRB and therefore tax liability at second death. Run through the below flow chart to work out how it might apply to your situation.

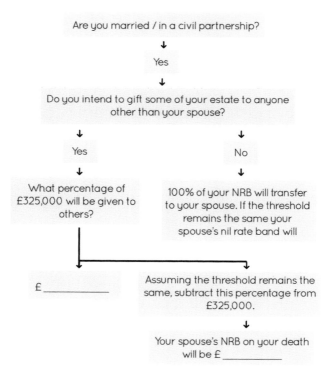

Are you married / in a civil partnership?

↓

Yes

↓

Do you intend to gift some of your estate to anyone other than your spouse?

↓ Yes   ↓ No

What percentage of £325,000 will be given to others?

100% of your NRB will transfer to your spouse. If the threshold remains the same your spouse's nil rate band will

£ _____   Assuming the threshold remains the same, subtract this percentage from £325,000.

↓

Your spouse's NRB on your death will be £ _____

5.2.2 Residential Nil Rate Band

Early in 2016 George Osborne announced plans for a new allowance, the residential nil rate band (RNRB). From April 2020 this will be fully in place, aiming to reduce inheritance tax for homeowners passing their family home down to their children. This will be phased in from April 2017, starting at £100,000 per person, increasing incrementally by £25,000 each year until 2020 when it will be set at £175,000, and will have the same carry forward rules as the NRB.

Provided you own a house, the RNRB will be added to your NRB to increase the amount that is free of inheritance tax. In 2020, a married couple with a house, on death, will have two allowances of NRB at £325,000 each and two allowances of RNRB at £175,000 each. In total you would have £1m free from tax liability.

Of course, while the positive aspects of the RNRB were announced, the small print was not; there are some caveats. Firstly, the RNRB is only available if the benefits from the family home are passed on to children - including stepchildren and foster children - grandchildren, or remoter issue. It could also be passed to a lifetime interest trust where the beneficiaries are any of the above. Other family members or friends can benefit from your NRB, but not from the RNRB.

Secondly, if the net value of your estate (including all assets excluded from inheritance tax under allowances) exceeds £2m, then for every £2 over this £2m, you will lose £1 of the RNRB - more tax will be payable. For example, a couple whose estate was worth £2.7m or more would get no RNRB at all.

If you are unsure whether you'd qualify for RNRB, run through the flowchart below.

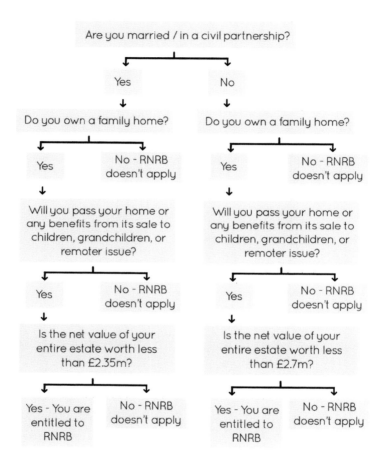

5.2.3 The 7-Year Rule

When calculating your inheritance tax liability you must also remember the 7-Year Rule: this rule states that, when someone dies, you add back into their estate any gifts that were made in the previous 7 years. The rule also states that gifts count towards the inheritance tax threshold before anything else in the estate. In other words, if you were to gift £32,500 and then die within 7 years, 10% of your nil rate band would have already been used up.

The value of any gift which exceeds your tax-free allowances, e.g. if you gifted £425,000, so £100,000 exceeds the nil rate band, becomes a PET (a potentially exempt transfer, not your pet cat!). In our example, the first £325,000 of the gift would be exempt from tax, but on the remaining £100,000 tax is liable - that is, until you have survived for 7 years after the gifting date.

The key feature of PETs is that over the course of the 7 years following the date of your gift there is tapering relief on the inheritance tax that would be liable were you to die at any point along that timeline, as follows:

Year	Discount
7	80%
6	60%
5	40%
4	20%
3	0
2	0
1	0

The percentage in the above table relates to the proportion of inheritance tax that would be discounted. For example, coming back to our PET worth £100,000: the tax due in the first 3 years would be £40,000, but if you were to die in year 5 you would receive a 40% discount on that £40,000, so the inheritance tax due would in fact be £24,000. In year 8 there is no inheritance tax on the amount of the gift. The transfer becomes exempt.

One final thing to remember is that, if you do not survive the gift by 7 years, the tax payable is the responsibility of the beneficiary!

EXERCISE
Complete A Simple Inheritance Tax Calculation

As a working example, calculate the inheritance tax that is payable on your estate as it stands at present.

Add the values of the following assets:

Your home	£_____
Other property	£_____
Your contents and cars	£_____
Your investments	£_____
Your pensions	£_____
Life insurance	£_____
Death in service	£_____
Total	£_____
Deduct	
Mortgage	£_____

Loans	£ _____
Total	£ _____
Less	**£ 325,000**
Net taxable estate	£ _____@ **40%**

Please note: this figure will change because your estate will change, and because tax rules regularly change.

Now take your net taxable estate and add to it your possible inheritance.

Net taxable estate	£_____
Possible inheritance	£_____
Total possible estate	£_____
Deduct £325,000	
Possible taxable estate	£_____@ **40%**
	£_____

The above calculations will give you an idea of the impact that inheriting can have on your estate. The inheritances that you will receive should be passed and processed in the right way so that they do not fall into your taxable estate.

5.2.4 Exemptions And Allowances

There are other tax free exemptions and allowances which will need to be taken into consideration when calculating your inheritance tax: we cover these in detail in Chapter 6.

Chapter 6
Allowances & Gifting

A key element of inheritance tax that can often be overlooked is that it is liable not only on the net value of your estate in the Will, but also on gifts made in your lifetime. You might wonder what business it is of the HMRC whether you've given money to your loved ones while still alive, and clients often ask us "Who's going to even know if I've made a gift?", but unfortunately HMRC have every right to look into it and charge you the liable tax.

Having said all that, there are some tax allowances on gifts. Knowing these allowances will help you to develop a gifting strategy so that you can mitigate the amount of inheritance tax due after your death. The two largest, which were covered in Chapter 5, are the nil rate band and the residential nil rate band which comes into effect in 2017. This chapter covers day-to-day allowances, annual allowances, some special one-off situations, and gives advice on what your strategy for gifting should be while still alive.

6.1 Allowances

6.1.1 Small Gifts

The small gift allowance means that there is no inheritance tax on individual gifts worth up to £250. You can give as many different people as you like up to £250 each in any one tax year (it resets every April). You can't, however, give someone another tax-free £250 if you've given them a gift using a different exemption, e.g. the £3,000 annual exemption (Section 6.1.3).

Also, after giving someone a tax-free £250 gift you cannot then give them a further gift in the same tax year. If you do then the whole amount is liable for tax: the first £250 is not exempt.

For example, if you gave your niece a gift of £250, this would be exempt from tax. However, if you subsequently gave her another £1,000 in the same tax year, then not only would tax be liable on the £1,000, it would also be liable on the £250. It now counts as part of a larger gift of £1,250.

6.1.2 Wedding Gifts

A second inheritance tax exemption is on gifts given for a wedding or civil partnership. The gift must be given on or shortly before the date of the wedding and the allowance is larger for your children's and grandchildren's weddings, but it also covers gifts to anyone getting married, specifically:

£5,000 given to a child
£2,500 given to a grandchild or great-grandchild
£1,000 given to anyone else.

The term 'gift' here also covers, say, a parent paying for their child's wedding. If you were to pay for your daughter's wedding, which cost £40,000, then the first £5000 of this would not count towards your estate for inheritance tax. The other £35,000 would be liable.

It's also important to note that you can only use this allowance once per beneficiary. If your daughter were to divorce and remarry, any wedding gift you gave her for the second marriage would be liable for inheritance tax.

6.1.3 Annual Exemption

A third allowance is called the 'annual exemption', and it means that the estate of the giftor, in the event of their death, does not have to pay inheritance tax on up to £3,000 worth of gifts they gave away - to anyone - in each tax year. In addition the exemption can be carried over from one tax year to the next, though the maximum exemption allowed in any one year is £6,000 (i.e. you may only carry over a single year's worth of allowance). As a simple example, say you did not use your annual gift allowance in one tax year; the following year you would be able to give your three children £2,000 each.

The annual exemption is separate from the small gift and marriage allowances, e.g. if you give your three children a small gift of £250 each, you would still have the full £3000 annual allowance to gift to someone else exempt from inheritance tax (in the case of the marriage allowance you would be able to give both the marriage gift allowance and annual allowance to the same person).

6.1.4 Gifts From Income

Where gifts are made from genuine income sources, and those gifts are both regular and do not affect the quality of the giftor's life, the value of the gift is exempt from tax. The term 'regular' usually means that the gift must have been made at least twice. Having said that, we have managed on occasions to demonstrate that there was an intention to gift regularly.

As mentioned, these gifts from income must not cause a reduction in the quality of living for the giftor. This means that you must have some form of documentation on file that demonstrates how your money is spent and that there is excess income to be gifted away regularly.

It may seem obvious, but gifts from income must come from an income source, not capital. If you had some form of investment bond that pays you the annual 5% allowance (check with your financial advisers about this type of product) the 5% payment is not defined as income. As a general rule, unless its income from an ISA, the gift must come specifically from taxed income to qualify.

6.1.5 Potentially Exempt Transfers

Any gifts given in your lifetime become part of your estate, and any which exceed the above allowances are liable for inheritance tax. Specifically, they become potentially exempt transfers (PETs). We discussed the '7-Year Rule' in Section 5.2.3 in terms of the calculation of your estate's net worth, but it's also important to think of PETs as a form of gifting allowance.

Remember that after 7 years, any gifts given no longer count towards your estate, and so are not liable for tax, and that before then PETs are subject to tapering tax relief. You might well want to consider, then, gifting earlier rather than later.

PETs can be a significant allowance, because there is no cap on the amount you can gift in your lifetime that would be excluded from inheritance tax after 7 years. As a quick example, if you had enough net worth to gift away £1m, say to your daughter, then around £675,000 of that gift would be liable for tax - so £270,000 would be payable in the event of your death - but if you survived for 7 years then no inheritance tax would be liable at all. Compared to leaving that £1m to your daughter in your Will, you've saved £270,000.

Another story in the news in 2015 was about a gift David Cameron's mother gave to him of £200,000 after his father died and left him £300,000 in his Will - not only did they save on the inheritance tax on his father's estate by dividing it this way, but also the gift of £200,000 from his mother will now fall outside her estate should she survive it by 7 years.[9] Again, we should emphasise that there is nothing wrong with this kind of estate planning to mitigate inheritance tax, but you may need to be careful if you are a politician in an election year!

6.1.6 Other Forms Of Relief

There are some other inheritance tax reliefs which allow

---

9 See for example this story in the Daily Mail: www.dailymail.co.uk/news/article-3531822/ Cameron-s-tax-bill-dodge-mother-s-200-000-gift-New-row-historic-decision-publish-PM-s-tax-return-revealed-family-avoided-70-000-bill-father-died.html

specific assets to be passed on free of tax liability: these include Business Relief, Agricultural Relief and Woodland Relief. A brief overview of each of these can be found below, but you should consult with a professional for full details and the conditions for application, and to see if you might qualify for any other kind of exemption.

6.1.6.1 Business Relief

This is aimed mainly at family businesses; the government allows you to pass businesses down through your family, generation after generation, in order for that business not to have to close just to pay tax liabilities. The relief effectively reduces the value of the business assets (in the eyes of the tax collector), including property etc., by either 50% or 100%, depending on circumstances, so that you end up paying either half or none of the tax.

The exception to this rule is investment businesses. Let's say your business was purely buy to let properties. You couldn't claim Business Relief for this because essentially all you're doing is holding those assets in a company to avoid other tax liabilities.

Another important point to note is that to qualify for Business Relief there must not be excessive cash holdings in a company, but only the amount of cash that is required 'for normal business cash flow purposes'. If it exceeds this level then the relief will not be allowed.

6.1.6.2 Agricultural Relief

Similar to Business Relief, Agricultural Relief allows you to reduce the value of property that is specifically used for farming (again, in the eyes of the taxman) by either 50% or 100% depending on circumstances. The property must have been occupied by the testator by at least two years prior to death to apply for this relief.

6.1.6.3 Woodland Relief

Woodland Relief, similar to the two exemptions above, can help reduce inheritance tax by allowing you to avoid including certain assets in the estate, in this case the value of the timber on your woodland. Although you must include the value of the woodland itself in the estate, if you qualify for Woodland Relief you only pay inheritance tax on the trees when they're sold or gifted away as timber. Note that you won't receive Woodland Relief if the woodland also qualifies for Agricultural or Business Relief.

6.1.7 Charities

Gifting to charities, museums, universities, community amateur sports clubs - any organisation with a registered charity number - in your lifetime is straightforward enough: these gifts fall outside of your estate automatically and so are not liable for tax. Things get a little more complicated, however, with charitable gifts left in the Will. These gifts are also not liable for inheritance tax, but significantly they can help you to reduce your overall inheritance tax liability. If you give away at least 10% of your net estate (i.e. after allowances etc.) to charity, the liability on the remaining estate drops from 40% to 36%.

It's important to note that this reduction in tax liability only applies if you are leaving gifts to charity in your Will. If you gave £100,000 to a charity just before you died, this would have no effect on the rate of inheritance tax you would pay after death. It's highly recommended, therefore, to allow your Will to do your charitable giving for you; as long as the combined charitable donation in your Will is at least 10% of your net estate you could make a big saving in terms of inheritance tax.

6.2 Your Gifting Strategy

Having worked out exactly what you can give away without incurring inheritance tax, let's now think about how and when to gift. Firstly, as long as you have enough money to do so, you should be making full use of all the allowances outlined above to give away your money as often and as early as possible to reduce your inheritance tax liability, that is a given. But past that, what should your strategy be?

To answer this question you'll first need answers to the following two questions:

1. Who is going to get the money?
2. Why should they not have that money now?

If you are worth say £2m, your house is worth £1m, you have £500,000 in a pension coming in, you have £500,000 in flexible assets and that gives you enough income, what is the point of waiting until your death to pass it down? Why are you forcing your children or grandchildren or other heirs to wait until your death before they receive this legacy you've built up, quite possibly increasing the tax liability by doing so?

There are very legitimate reasons for this. You might actually need the money yourself now, or expect to need it in the future for nursing care or similar costs. Or perhaps the assets are tied up, say as the controlling shares in a company, which you wouldn't be willing to gift to your children and thereby lose control of the company. There are many reasons, and yet two of the most common are less tangible. First, clients are often very attached to their money and are unwilling to give it up, and second, they are concerned that the beneficiary will misuse the money they gift.

The first reason can be difficult for many clients to circumvent. We spend around 80% of our lives in acquisition mode, building up our assets, and we get used to that way of living. But as we get older we need to move into disbursal mode, distributing those assets we have built up either to others, or spending them for ourselves. The second reason can be a genuine concern: we want to retain control over our money when we think the beneficiary will waste it. However, remember that after your death, you have no control whatsoever. If the beneficiary is going to misuse the money now, they will probably misuse it once you've passed away.

Trusts can be a solution to this problem, and we'll discuss the relative merits of direct gifting vs gifting via a trust in Section 6.2.3, and also go into trusts in detail in Chapter 7. Hopefully by the end of this chapter you'll be convinced that neither of these is a good reason to delay gifting until the Will.

Now, having considered who you'll gift to and whether you could in fact remove the assets from your estate sooner rather than later, let's get into the detail of creating your strategy: what should you give, when, and how.

Note: Don't Forget, You Can Spend Your Money Too!

Although we've been talking a lot about gifting, don't forget that you can spend your money too. Remember that all of your estate over the tax-free threshold will be liable for 40% tax. Think of it this way: spending £5,000 as you grow older is more like spending £3,000, because if that money had fallen into your estate after death, HMRC would have collected £2,000 of it!

A few years ago one of our clients was a couple in their 70s, worth around £1.8m and living in a very comfortable house, their income more or less equalling their outgoings. In one of our meetings they mentioned that their computer wasn't working very well, so we asked why they didn't go and buy a new one. The husband John's immediate response was, "Do you know how much computers cost now?

They're around £600." When we asked him how much their investments had gone up that year he replied, "£10,000." They couldn't get over the idea that spending £600 was a great deal of money, despite their perfectly lucrative situation. When they came back for another meeting the next year, they still had the same dodgy computer which kept crashing on them. After John again exclaimed that it was "A lot of money!", we asked him, "Compared to what?"

Finally, in the third year, their lives had significantly improved because they'd bought a new computer which worked. They didn't spend all their time trying to fix it talking to an IT helpline, and a major source of stress had been removed.

It can be difficult to get out of aquisition mode, but as you grow older you should try to worry less about making money and enjoy life!

6.2.1 How Much Is Enough?

When considering how much to gift away in your lifetime, remember that from an estate planning perspective the ideal situation you want to achieve is to be below all inheritance tax thresholds at the time of your death.

Of course, the question then is: when are you going to die? It's impossible to know for sure, but we can assume none of us will live to 120. It's unlikely we'll live to 110, but it's possible. You'll have to make an educated guess as to what age you think you'll live to, and so work out how much money you'll need for that time. Once you've made a decision, this will not only help shape your gifting strategy, but also your investment strategy: if you know how long your money has to last for, you'll know how much money you need to make, and so what level of risk you'll need to take.[10]

You should bear in mind, however, that the vast majority of our clients overestimate their needs by a large margin, and die far too wealthy. Relying solely on a clever Will is not going to mitigate much inheritance tax at all. You must begin to take action long before death. You must also try to accept that your estate will reduce or erode over time in order to get it below the taxable thresholds; a man or woman used to saying, "I'm worth £3m" can find it difficult to adjust to, "Actually I'm now worth £900,000". But ask yourself, when you're 99 years old, do you really need all of that £3m?

The question, then, of how much you should gift away, has a relatively straightforward answer. Gift as much as possible to minimise inheritance tax, once you have worked out what you will need to live as you'd like in your latter years, with some leeway in case of unforeseen circumstances.

---

10 For much more detail on investment strategy read David's book The 17 Mistakes Investors Make.

6.2.2 Should You Gift Directly Or Via A Trust?

So you should now have an idea of exactly how much you'd like to gift away to help mitigate inheritance tax. But how to do so? The two main methods for gifting are to directly hand over the asset, or to gift via a trust. There are some pros and cons to each, mostly dependent on the size of the gift, which we'll look at now.

Direct gifting, quite simply, is quick and straightforward. There's no admin and no cost, which naturally there is in setting up a trust, and if your direct gift exceeds the tax-free threshold it becomes a potentially exempt transfer, with tapering tax relief over 7 years should you die within that time period (see Section 5.2.3 for more detail on the 7-Year Rule). For any small gift (a few thousand pounds or less) it will probably make most sense to simply directly gift it.

There is a serious drawback to direct gifting, however: once you hand over a direct gift to the beneficiary, you lose all control over it. This is why, especially for large gifts, trusts are so useful: it's possible to set up trusts in various ways, retaining various levels of control over the assets. For a situation where, say, you have £500,000 which you have no need for, and would never have a need for, you might wish to gift it to your two children.

Unfortunately, you suspect they might misuse it. They might not be sensible, buying new cars instead of paying off the mortgage, or perhaps you think it would make them lose their ambition. These are all very valid reasons to avoid direct gifting. What we might recommend in this situation is to gift the £500,000 to a trust which would hold it on behalf of the children, so that when the time comes you could release the money from the trust to them. Not only will this money fall outside your estate 7 years after setting up the trust, but you also retain control.

The admin and costs associated with setting up the trust, and any tax due on it, will usually pale in comparison with the importance of retaining control over the assets. One caveat to be aware of is that, unlike with direct gifting, there is no tapering tax relief on a gift given via many trusts. Rather than a potentially exempt transfer, the gift is categorised as a lifetime chargeable transfer, and if you were to die within 7 years of giving it the full 40% inheritance tax would be liable.

We'll look at trusts in more detail in Chapter 7, but essentially for a large gift there is no real reason not to use a trust, and you should set it up as soon as possible to avoid incurring non-tapering tax on the lifetime chargeable transfer should you die within 7 years. Direct gifting, on the other hand, makes more sense with small gifts.

The Role Of Trusts

In reading this book you'll have come across the term 'trust' several times so far. You may already have some understanding of what a trust is, or you may not. You may also have heard many scary things about trusts - how expensive they are, how complex they are to administer, how they tie up your assets - all of which can be true, if they are not set up correctly or are not managed correctly. Either way we would encourage you to read this chapter, as trusts are a key tool in estate planning and can be very complex, so it certainly wouldn't hurt to refresh your memory or to fill any gaps in knowledge! As well as outlining what trusts are, we'll cover when you should and shouldn't be using them, and what the tax implications of using a trust can be.

So, what exactly is a trust? In simple terms, a trust is just a legal vehicle that allows one person to hold assets (which can be almost anything) to which another person is entitled, while the trust itself technically 'owns' them - we've found that one of the best analogies to illustrate this is a buying a round at the bar.

Say you are at the pub with two friends, Kat and Brad. It's your round, but you need to run to the bathroom. You might give £20 to Kat and ask her to buy drinks for you all - a lager, a gin and tonic and a white wine. You've now created a trust. It's an oral trust, not very enforceable under the law, but still a trust. There are three parties to every trust: the settlor who creates it, the trustee who holds the assets, and the beneficiaries who benefit from the trust.

In this case you are the settlor, as you gave the £20 to Kat; Kat is the trustee, as she's holding the money while she goes to the bar; and all three of you are the beneficiaries, because you all get drinks from the £20 in the trust. Remember that, just like choosing your executor, choosing your trustee should be a very carefully thought out decision, as they are in charge of looking after that money.

In this case the settlor benefits from the trust too, as you get a drink along with Kat and Brad. These are called settlor-interested trusts, because the person who created it still has an interest in the assets within the trust. Unfortunately settlors who retain access to the assets in a trust do not avoid inheritance tax, as the assets still fall within their estate. If you wanted to avoid the taxman getting hold of their 40% share of your £20 trust, you'd have to ask Kat to buy drinks for herself and Brad but not for you.

You'll hopefully now have a basic understanding of how a trust works, so let's look at some of the different types available.

7.1 Types Of Trust

Before your advisor can help you to decide which type of trust to set up, you - as the settlor - should work out what you want the trust to do. Firstly, do you want to have any access to the assets in the trust (i.e. should the trust be settlor-interested)? Perhaps you want the growth of the capital to fall outside your estate while retaining access, or you want to gift the capital while retaining the income it gives you? Or perhaps you simply want to gift the whole asset away? Secondly, you should decide what access the beneficiaries should have, and when they should be able to access it (as well as who they should be). Finally you should work out the level of control you'd like the trustees to have in looking after the trust.

You may well not have an exact idea of what you want yet, and your advisor can help you to work this out, but once a general outline of the purpose of the trust has been drawn, you will usually be advised to set up one of the following three types.

7.1.1 Bare Trust

A bare trust, or absolute trust, is the most straightforward of the three. Once you, the settlor, gift an asset into a bare trust, you can no longer access any part of that asset. It falls outside your estate, but it also means that there is very little flexibility on who can benefit. Only the named beneficiary has any claim on the asset or any growth that asset achieves.

The main use of this kind of trust is gifting to minors (under 18 in the UK): you want to avoid gifting in your Will because of inheritance tax, you want to avoid direct gifting because a young person will most likely not use that money wisely, but you also want to ensure that they receive the money eventually.

This gives you greater control than simply handing them the money, but once they turn 18 the beneficiary has every right to take that money out of the trust and use it how they wish. To retain more control you'll want to use either a discretionary trust or an interest in possession trust.

7.1.2 Discretionary Trust

Discretionary trusts are the most flexible of the three types discussed here: as the name suggests it gives discretion to the trustees to decide how to distribute the assets; how much discretion will depend on how the trust is set up. Also, unlike a bare trust, a discretionary trust can be set up as settlor-interested. In fact there is a great deal of flexibility in who the beneficiaries can be, as the trust can name 'classes' of beneficiary rather than specific individuals (e.g. "nephews and nieces, current or future", leaving it up to the trustees to decide who should benefit), and what conditions might need to be met for those beneficiaries to inherit from the trust. Depending on the trust deed, trustees can decide:

- what gets paid out (income or capital)
- which beneficiary to make payments to
- how often payments are made
- any conditions to impose on the beneficiaries

Coming back to our bar example, if you - the settlor - thought that neither of your friends Kat or Brad would do a good job going to the bar (i.e. looking after the assets in the trust) you could set yourself up as the trustee. You would go to the bar yourself, and, with a discretionary trust, could decide exactly when Kat and Brad would get their drinks, and what kind of drinks they should get, if any.

Discretionary trusts are often used to put aside assets for a future beneficiary - perhaps a grandchild who has not yet been born but will most likely need the money more than your children or spouse if they are - or to keep control over assets intended for beneficiaries who are deemed not capable or responsible enough to deal with the money themselves.

We sometimes have clients coming into the office worried sick about one of their children who is not at all responsible with money and spends recklessly. Our advice to them will usually be something along these lines: set up a trust whereby the trustees give their child a regular allowance, perhaps if the child meets certain conditions such as getting a job, but ensuring that child has no access to the actual assets in the trust themselves.

Another example of how useful discretionary trusts can be is the fact that the trustees can loan money to anyone who complies with whatever is specified in the trust deed. Say you - as the trustee - loaned £10,000 to your niece; if she were to get divorced, her former husband would have no claim on the loaned money, because it is not technically hers. Equally were she to die before paying it back that money would not count as part of her estate and therefore in the inheritance tax calculation. The £10,000 would come out of her estate and back to the trust.

As we have seen, then, discretionary trusts can be a very powerful tool and have many uses. We have only covered a few here, so be sure to seek out advice on how you should set yours up.

7.1.3 Interest In Possession Trust

An interest in possession (IIP) trust is used when you - as the settlor - would like someone other than the intended beneficiary to actually benefit from the trust before the beneficiary inherits it. This person would have no claim on owning the assets within the trust, but they might, say, be paid an allowance from the income it earns. This type of trust is often used to protect your assets, and to ensure that the intended beneficiaries receive exactly what you want them to (see Chapter 10 for more on protecting your assets), without entirely excluding a third party from access.

For example, let's say you were getting married for the second time, and both you and your husband already have children of your own. You both bring £200,000 worth of assets into the marriage, and buy a house together. You want to ensure that, after your death, the value of your half of the house is passed to your own children, and to do so you could set up an IIP trust for that half of the house.

The trust would specify that your husband is free to use (i.e. live in) your half of the house after your death, but on his death it would pass to your children rather than to him. Had you simply left everything to him in your Will, he would be free to choose what to do with that half of the house. If he wanted to he could simply give everything to his own children. IIPs, then, can be very useful for carrying out your wishes.

We should also note that IIPs can be set up as a settlor-interested trust. You are able to gift the asset to remove it from your estate (losing its liability after 7 years), while still retaining an income from it - see Chapter 8 for details.

7.2 Use Of Trusts

7.2.1 When Should You Use A Trust?

Trusts are the most powerful way to protest assets on death. They can be used to legally reduce inheritance tax, to avoid assets falling into probate for months on end, and to protect inheritances from divorce, bankruptcy or separation. We went over some specific situations where trusts can be useful in Section 7.1, and we go into much more detail on protecting your assets in Chapter 8, but generally there are several reasons for setting up trusts: the first is to reduce inheritance tax, the second is to make sure that the assets and money in the trusts pass to the right person at the right time.

Trusts are often also used to take advantage of changes in legislation, for example, the new RNRB coming into effect in 2017 would be reduced if the estate exceeds £2m. They can also be used to obtain a third NRB. It's also important to note that, although we advise on setting up trusts in your lifetime, most people will still need some form of trust written into their Will; you should not solely rely on the Will to carry out your wishes.

There's a reason why so many wealthy people use trusts. It ensures the money goes to the right person at the right time. It doesn't get eroded through taxation. It doesn't get lost in divorce. If you're passing down £1m to your children, would you want to risk that getting lost? Your daughter might marry the son-in-law from hell - would you want him to take half of that £1m, when for a couple of thousand pounds you could protect everything using a trust arrangement? Hopefully these questions answer themselves!

7.2.2 When Should You Create The Trust?

So, armed with the knowledge that trusts are a good idea, you may now be wondering when you should set yours up. Many people avoid putting trusts in place because they find them scary or too complicated. However, our advice is that a trust should be created as soon as you believe you'll have a need for it in the future; you should never wait until the trust is actually needed to create it. Set it up, register it with HMRC, and put it in place prior to its use.

The reason for this is that legislation and regulation on trusts changes so regularly, the last thing you want is for the rules to be changed before you have a chance to set it up. If, for example, you're planning to create a trust to gift money to your children, don't wait until you have the money available. Set up the trust as soon as possible and simply place the money into it when it becomes available.

7.2.2 When Should You Not Use A Trust?

This section will be fairly short and sweet: you probably get the sense by now that for any large sum of money, it's a very good idea to use a trust. So when should you not use one? Essentially, when the gift you'd like to give is too small to be worth it (see Section 6.2.2); when the only reason for using the trust is to avoid inheritance tax on an asset but you doubt you'll survive for 7 years after gifting it (although inter vivos life insurance can cover the tax liability); or in the handful of situations where the specific asset you'd like to gift cannot be held in a trust. Otherwise, go ahead and set the trust up, as soon as possible!

7.3 Taxation

The best way to think about taxation on a trust is that generally a trust will be taxed in the same way that a person is. There are some taxes for paying into a trust, some for paying out of it, and some liable while the trust is holding your asset. For example, if there's an asset in the trust that generates income, income tax will be charged on the income. If there is an asset in the trust and that asset is sold, it may be liable for capital gains tax. Like a person, trusts have an allowance for income tax and capital gains tax.

The tax rates and allowances change almost yearly and so we will not cover them here; you should take a look at the HMRC website to establish the present rates and allowances if you are going to use a trust.

Some trusts have additional taxation, such as the 'periodic charge' on discretionary trusts. This applies to assets in excess of the nil rate band, and is charged every 10 years after the trust is set up (currently at 6% every 10 years, which equates to 0.6% a year). As far as we're concerned, this tax is so small the benefits of using a discretionary trust will massively outweigh it, and this is true of most forms of taxation on trusts, the obvious exception being inheritance tax.

Having said all that, the taxation of trusts is incredibly complex. So much so that most financial advisors don't understand it, and relatively few accountants come close to having an understanding of it. The rules change not only under legislation and regulation, but also via precedents. You should seek individual, professional assistance with regards to any trust that you're looking to use and the resulting tax implications outside of inheritance tax. It would not be possible to cover even a fraction of the content necessary in this book.

Chapter 8
Techniques For Avoidance

Before writing this chapter we added up the number of possible ways to avoid and mitigate inheritance tax when planning your estate, and the total came to 97. Obviously we are not going to list all 97 of them here, as that would require a book in itself (and not a very interesting one at that!), but we'll outline the top five most commonly used techniques. Whatever your circumstances you will most likely use one or two of these, together with a handful of some of the methods not listed that will be more specific to your individual situation.

Please note, the following techniques have been simplified for the purposes of this book, to demonstrate the type of arrangements which are possible. Again, these do not form any formal advice, and the full details and structure of these have not been included to keep the book manageable and understandable.

You should seek professional advice from a STEP practitioner, estate planning specialist or chartered financial planner to understand how each of these might be relevant in your own circumstances, and to receive advice on the other techniques.

8.1 Inheritance Tax And Pensions

In the UK, the vast majority of people have a pension arrangement which forms a significant part of their estate. In the event of their death, prior to age 75, if the pension passes to their spouse or to their children, under present regulations there is no inheritance tax. However, when those assets are then passed to the next surviving beneficiary on second death, inheritance tax becomes liable.

For example, most couples will leave their pension money to each other, not to their children, because the surviving spouse needs the money. If you were to die and leave everything to your wife, she will receive all that money free of tax. But when your wife then dies, that money from the pension forms part of her estate, and so when she passes it down to your children there's an inheritance tax charge. Pension funds, therefore, are usually taxed when they're passed down to the next generation.

A way to avoid this tax liability is to set up what's called a spousal bypass trust. You make the trust the beneficiary of the pension, rather than the spouse, and the trust then passes the assets down at second death. In the example above, rather than the pension money falling into your wife's estate on your death, the money would fall into the trust. You could then make her the beneficiary of that trust, so that she can access the money and receive an income, but then when she dies she isn't actually leaving any money to your children.

The trust itself passes the money down to them, because you would have named them as the second line of beneficiaries (the remaindermen). This incurs no tax liability. Solely using a spousal bypass, for most people, will make a significant saving in their inheritance tax.

Of course, this is a simplified explanation of the situation because 'pension freedom' has made many changes to what happens to pensions on death. It has also created a difference in the way pensions are treated prior to age 75 and after age 75. It is therefore important to think about your estate planning in the context of your pension planning. This probably means that you should obtain pension advice at the same time as obtaining estate planning advice.

8.2 Life Insurance

The second technique works in a similar way. Most people in the UK have some form of life insurance or death in service benefit. As a quick illustrative example: say you had life insurance of £300,000. On your death you could pass that money tax-free to your wife or children, but just like with a pension this money would fall into their estate on their death, incurring inheritance tax.

The way around this is to set up an assurance trust, which collects the benefits of life insurance. Just like with the pension technique given in the previous section, the trust is made the beneficiary of the insurance, and your spouse or children can then be made the beneficiary of the trust. This keeps the money from falling into anyone's estate, and so avoids incurring inheritance tax at second death.[11]

Note: Inter Vivos Life Insurance

At this point we should also mention 'inter vivos' life insurance, as it too can be used to avoid inheritance tax, specifically on PETs or lifetime chargeable transfers. Inter vivos (which in Latin means 'between people') insurance covers the tax liability on a gift made in the last 7 years of your life (see Section 5.2.3 for the 7-Year Rule); in other words, this kind of insurance will pay out whatever inheritance tax is due on the gift in the event of your death before 7 years have passed.

If you are planning to make a large gift, and are perhaps concerned that you won't survive it by the full 7 years, an inter vivos policy could be a good choice to essentially nullify the inheritance tax due on that gift.

8.3 Property Gifting And Retained Income Trusts

A common investment strategy in the UK is into rental properties, and while this may well be sensible from an investment point of view, it is less so from the point of view of inheritance tax.

---

11 The same is true with death in service benefits, but current UK legislation dictates they must pass to an asset preservation trust rather than an insurance trust. The asset preservation trust is specifically designed to collect death in service benefits from employers.

This is because when you die, should you pass the rental property on to anyone other than your spouse (which only delays the issue until her death), inheritance tax will be payable on the equity in the property. If there is a mortgage on the property, however, this will reduce the equity and hence also the inheritance tax payable. Therefore, a higher level of debt on an investment property is a good thing from an inheritance tax point of view. There is also a further benefit, because the interest payable on that debt is a tax deduction, and will thus reduce any income tax on the income generated.

Anyone with a residential portfolio should consider moving a proportion of that portfolio into a retained income trust. A retained income trust will allow you to retain the income from the property of the trust, while ensuring that part of that property falls outside of the estate for inheritance tax purposes. At present the maximum proportion you can move into the trust is 50%.

Say you have a property portfolio valued at £100,000, and that generates £10,000 worth of income in rent. If you transferred the maximum 50% of your portfolio - in this example, £50,000 - into the retained income trust, you would still retain 100% of the £10,000 income a year, but you now pay half the inheritance tax. Placing property into a retained income trust is one of the few ways that you can legally have your cake and eat it too. Usually this type of arrangement would be considered a 'gift with reservation'.

A gift with reservation means that you cannot retain any

benefit on any asset given away. If you do the value of the gift will be retained in your estate for inheritance tax purposes. The present HMRC view that up to 50% of this kind of asset can be passed into the trust, with all of the income being retained, is quite unusual, and one that may not be in place for much longer. Indeed, if we were to remove certain HMRC approvals, this would be one. When transferring assets into this type of trust you must also consider any other implications such as stamp duty or capital gains tax, either of which might be generated by such a transfer.

There are various different types of retained income trust, and each is specific to the type of asset it will contain; not only property, but any income-generating asset can be transferred into one. Generally speaking the level of income that will be paid to the settlor is agreed when the trust is established, and it's also agreed with the HMRC. That income is then paid regularly and never varies. You must also be sure that you do not need access to the capital you transfer into the trust before you do so, as the settlor cannot access it at all.

8.4 Discretionary Settlements

The fourth technique is, again, similar to some of those above, in that it sets up a trust - in this case a discretionary settlement[12] - as the beneficiary of assets after death rather than the spouse or children. A discretionary trust can be used for most assets not covered by the above techniques, and in just the same

---

12 A discretionary settlement is a form of discretionary trust, and the terms are often interchangeable. For the purposes of our explanation discretionary settlement can mean discretionary trust and vice versa.

way it allows the assets to fall outside of your family's estate at second death.

This is particularly relevant with the implementation of the new residential nil rate band: if your assets are in excess of £2m, for every £2 they exceed that threshold, you will lose £1 of the RNRB allowance (see Section 5.2.2). Therefore, say you are worth £1.2m and your wife is worth £1m: if you leave everything to her in the event of your death, she will now be worth £2.2m. Because of this, in the event of her death, her estate will lose £100,000 of the RNRB allowance. If, on the other hand, you left £200,000 of your estate to a discretionary trust, her estate would still qualify for the full RNRB which would mean saving £40,000 in inheritance tax. This small action can have a dramatic impact on the tax payable on death, while also simplifying probate on the second death.

Unfortunately, far too often we have seen non-specialist solicitors (and even some specialists) remove a trust on first death as 'it is not needed because there's no tax between spouses', so that the full value of the estate passes to the survivor, and all that careful estate planning is destroyed. Whenever a trust is involved it is therefore imperative that you seek the advice of someone who really knows what they are doing when it comes to probate, trusts and taxation.

Discretionary trusts can also allow the trustees some flexibility in choosing how to distribute the assets they have charge of. The settlor can set up conditions for who a potential beneficiary could be, so that, say, as-yet unborn grandchildren might be able to benefit in addition to the spouse and children.

It should be noted that there are many other functions for discretionary settlements, including, when used correctly, creating a third nil rate band with effective gifting. We won't cover this technique in the book as it is rather complicated and must be individually designed based upon the makeup of the estate. However, the principle involves moving part of the survivor's estate into a discretionary settlement following first death (usually part of the home) so that the transferred asset falls out of the estate on second death. If done correctly a third nil rate band can be created saving £130,000 of inheritance tax. A useful technique to be aware of!

8.5 Gift And Loan Arrangement

The final technique deals with the issue that, as your financial assets increase in value over time, so too will the inheritance tax on your estate. If, say, one of your investments grew from £200,000 to £250,000, your tax liability would also rise from £80,000 to £100,000. Effectively, 40% of the gain of your investments is always going to go to the government, unless you spend it or give it away.

One of the ways to negotiate this issue is by putting in place a gift and loan arrangement. This places your invested assets into a trust, under the terms of which you (the settlor) retain access to the capital. Any gains on the investments made within the trust, however, are outside of your estate and are owned by the trust.

Using the above example: if you placed your £200,000 investment into a gift and loan arrangement, and this grew to £250,000, you would have £250,000 in the trust but only £200,000 of its value pulling into your estate on death. The trust would own the extra £50,000, so the growth falls outside of your estate. This would allow you to keep your inheritance tax liability at the lower figure of £80,000, while still increasing your assets from £200,000 to £250,000.

The ideas and solutions noted above are just a small selection of the techniques that are available to reduce inheritance tax in ways approved by the HMRC, and are the most popular, as well as those which most good estate planners will understand and can implement.

One word of caution, however, is to ALWAYS seek written advice from anyone recommending trust arrangements. Far too many times have we seen people put arrangements in place without receiving written advice. Without this there is no protection if the arrangements go wrong, and unfortunately all too often they do go wrong. Remember the quality of the advice you receive is only ever as good as the written recommendations that you receive.

PART

3

Family

Chapter 9

Dangers Of Inheriting

When considering how to plan your estate and how and when to distribute your assets, a key factor that is far too often overlooked is how your beneficiaries (most likely your children) will deal with their inheritance. Time and again we have come across stories where an inheritance, or even the expectation of an inheritance, from a parent has had a quite serious negative impact on the life of a child; either that, or the assets end up being eroded through misspending or divorce.

This chapter highlights the potential dangers that come with leaving money to others, and includes a selection of stories from our own experience which should hopefully ensure that you go on to read Chapter 10, in which we'll give advice on protecting your assets and dealing with these potential pitfalls.

9.1 Expectation And Lack Of Ambition

One issue that crops up with inheritance is that, when a person inherits too young, or when they learn that eventually they will inherit £1m, £2m, £3m etc., they often lose their drive to push hard through life and to create their own success. They know that their financial future is secure so why would they bother saving money or even learning how to manage it? They blow all their money and don't build up their own asset base, so that they just become leeches on their parents' estate.

Although their parents most likely worked very hard to build up their assets, this is not always visible to the children. They see their parents go off to work but not what they're actually doing to provide for the family. We find that these cases are often made worse by a childhood where everything was provided without the child seeing where it actually came from. There's a danger they don't develop a sense of the value of money.

A middle-aged son of one of our clients, who was set to inherit a very large sum from his parents, had exactly this problem. He saw that money as his retirement fund, so in his lifetime he has floated along, built up debt, and expected his parents to bail him out on a regular basis. His view is that at some point he's going to inherit their wealth, so it's essentially his money anyway. Despite having a family of his own he has developed no sense of financial responsibility or ambition. We should therefore keep in mind that these are issues that don't solely affect young people.

Ironically, as children in their expectation of inheritance become more and more of a leech on their parents' estate, the less likely they might be to actually inherit! Another example we came across was of a couple in their 60s who had drafted their Will so that everything would be split between their two sons. A few years later, they came back into the office asking to redraft the Will. Their eldest son, safe in the knowledge that he would inherit plenty of money had been spending lavishly. The parents were worried that the £2m inheritance that would pass to him would disappear very quickly indeed, so they had decided to take away any control he'd had over the assets in the Will. His brother would receive half the estate, and the rest would be put into a trust for the family.

The eldest brother had no direct access to the money that he had been expecting. The parents made the youngest son a controlling trustee of the trust that held the money for the eldest son, and the parents' instructions to the trustees were to give priority to the children of the eldest son, rather than pass money to him directly.

The expectation of inheritance, then, can have a big impact on how a potential beneficiary lives their life. Closely related to this is the issue of misspending, which we'll look at now.

9.2 Misspending

One of the things that parents are almost always concerned about is that, when they pass money down to their children, the inheritance will be wasted on frivolous purchases, and that it won't be managed correctly. Most of our clients have built their assets over their whole life, and we find that once they've reached retirement, or whenever they stop working, they tend to be very careful with that money. They don't spend it on themselves, they don't do the things that perhaps they should do, because they want to pass it down to the children.

But when the children inherit, guess what they do? They are instead the ones who do the misspending. "Mum and Dad wouldn't go and travel," - because they wanted to pass the money on - "so I'm going to go and travel." Or, "Dad drove around in a 20-year-old banger; when I inherit, I'm going to buy an Aston Martin." This happens time, and time, and time again. After paying off any debt they might have, often a mortgage, the first thing that children tend to spend money on is a car. And not just any car either, it's almost always the car of their dreams. This might not be misspending in the technical sense, but a car is not an investment, and it's not the kind of thing the parents would have spent their money on, or wanted their children to spend it on.

We had a client come in to do her Will a couple of years ago; she was a twin, and their parents had died when they were relatively young. Her and her twin both inherited a reasonable amount of money - not a large amount, but at age 18 it most likely felt life-changing. One of the first questions we ask when drafting a Will, when there are children in the picture, is, "If you were to die today, at what age do you want your kids to benefit? To be able to spend it themselves, do with it what they like?"

This client immediately jumped in and said, "It's definitely 25 for me. Definitely 25." Usually people will say 18 or 21, so naturally we asked her why she wanted it to be so late, and she told us what had happened after she and her twin inherited at 18. She herself had continued with her education, gone to university and invested the money sensibly, so that it helped her buy her first property once she had begun her career. Her twin, on the other hand, felt that it was enough money to see her through life: she didn't continue with her education, and didn't invest the money. A few years down the line that money was no longer there for her. She took no financial advice and spent it quickly. When that money had run out, she didn't have the skills to go out and find a career and start earning money for herself again. You can see why the client wanted to set the age for her own kids to inherit at 25!

Note: Dealing With Expectation And Misspending

Although there are financial ways to deal with the issue of expectation and anticipated misspending, by, say, setting up a clever system of trusts so that your child receives a yearly allowance rather than a lump sum (and telling them so), it would be far preferable to prevent these issues arising. Ideally you want to be safe in the knowledge that however you gift your assets to your children, they will deal with them responsibly. The best way to ensure this, in our experience, is through education. Ideally you'd begin with them as young as possible, but they can still learn well into their 30s, 40s and beyond! Managing finances is a subject that is unfortunately not taught in most schools, so the responsibility for this does fall on parents. However, we consider it to be our responsibility to some extent as well.

We run a workshop each year called The Next-Generation workshop, which is for the children of our clients, explaining to them what they have to do when their parents die, and beforehand what they should do to prepare. In the 3-hour workshop, 1 hour is dedicated to preparing to inherit. No matter what the sum of money, it's important for them to know how to manage investments before that money comes into their hands. They'll learn that they should begin to structure their investments now, so that when that wealth is inherited there is a ready made system in place, in order for them to keep managing and investing that money. Hopefully after completing the workshop they will have less of an expectation that they can be financially lazy, and will not misspend their whole inheritance.

9.3 Divorce

Without a doubt the main concern clients walking through our door have over inheritance is divorce. Let's say you pass down £500,000 on your death to your child, who is married. If they then get divorced, that £500,000 must be included in the financial disclosure form for divorce. No matter where the assets came from, no matter what they consist of, if they belong to your child, then they would be a part of the marital finances and therefore would be up for grabs by the spouse. This is why divorce is such a big worry. No parent, who has spent their life scrimping and saving to build up an estate, wants to see their hard-earned money disappear out of the family. We've spent a lot of time discussing how to avoid inheritance tax at 40%, but with divorce 50% of your estate could be claimed by the ex-partner!

Divorce rates in the UK are currently around 48%: that means if you have two children, statistically speaking one of them will most likely get a divorce. The problem is that people never really think that it'll be them. A son- or daughter-in-law might be your favourite person in the world...right up until the point they divorce your child.

Not wanting to offend, presuming that a marriage will last, or assuming that the son- or daughter-in-law would never claim the inheritance you gifted, are all reasons that parents don't set up protection for the assets they pass down. But divorce is a messy business and money often becomes a key point of contention.

An example of this happened recently: a client had just inherited shares in her father's business, and came in to ask, "What happens if me and my husband get divorced, to these shares?" We told her, "Well, they're yours now, which means that if something happens to you and your husband and you get divorced, he has every right to make a claim on those assets." She was surprised that, even though the shareholding was within a family business, he had a right to make a claim on them. Unfortunately later they did indeed get a divorce, and the husband made a claim on the shares.

The main thing to remember, here, is that people are often overly romantic about marriage. Sons- and daughters-in-law can change dramatically, especially when large sums of money are involved, so it's best to be practical and plan ahead. A Beneficiary Protection Trust can be used as a legal vehicle that protects assets when they pass to a beneficiary, as we'll discover in Chapter 10. It is this type of trust that is perfect to protect assets from the divorce of a child. With careful drafting it can also be used to protect from misspending as well.

9.4 Remarriage

The last potential pitfall that we're going to discuss in this chapter is remarriage. Leaving everything to your spouse is common. But what if your spouse remarries after you die? What if their remarriage is a really bad idea? This is something people don't always consider: a large chunk of the assets you've built up over your lifetime, which you'd intended should go to your kids, could well end up leaving the family. Remember that marriage invalidates any previous Will.

If the surviving spouse does not get their Will updated, then the new partner will receive a substantial amount due to intestacy rules. Even worse, should their new marriage fail and end in divorce, an even greater proportion of your estate could be handed over to someone you never even knew.

We had one client, Shaun, in recent years whose wife passed away. She left him all of her half of their estate, around £1m, intending that their kids should get everything when he died. A few years after her death, Shaun took a trip to Asia and 'acquired' a new wife 30 years his junior, who is almost certainly going to outlive him, if they don't get divorced first. He updated his Will so that his new wife was a beneficiary along with the children, and while he is perfectly entitled to do so, it is quite likely not what his first wife would have wanted.

We should note that, while it is perfectly possible the same situation could occur if the husband died first - a widow might decide to marry a 'toy boy' - in our experience the reality is that women tend to make much more sensible choices when it comes to remarriage. Men often make rather poor choices in this area.

This issue of remarriage of the spouse following the first spouse's death is always a delicate one. Everyone believes - or at least hopes - that their spouse will do the right thing regarding assets following their death. But things change with time - we can't predict the future, and most importantly of all we can't predict who the surviving spouse will become involved with. Often it is the new 'boyfriend' or 'girlfriend' that has an influence. This can happen at any age, whether in your 40s or 90s.

Note: Long Term Care Costs

As we have seen, for a lot of people passing all their estate to a surviving spouse is absolutely the wrong thing to do. As well as remarriage, another issue to consider is the cost of long-term care.

If you and your wife are both alive and you become ill, your wife will most likely stay at home to look after you, meaning there are no additional care costs. However, if you then die and your wife becomes ill, you would not be there to look after her. In that case, the local authority may well be paying for her care. If you left your entire estate to her, the local authority would take that money to pay for the care. Essentially they will take out the cost of care from whatever assets the patient has. If, on the other hand, you had gifted your estate into a series of trusts, the local authority would not be able to use it, because it doesn't belong to her.

At this point you may be very concerned at the prospect of some of the situations described in the previous chapter! Although that wasn't entirely our intention, it is important to be aware of these problems and to plan practically around them. Many people think, "I want something simple. I should just pass everything to my spouse. I don't need to worry about it." Ok, sure. But if you pass it to the spouse now, what happens if the spouse remarries?

What happens if the spouse needs care? What happens to the lost allowance and the additional inheritance tax because you've passed it to them? And then they think, "Oh, well I just want to pass it all to the children then." Ok, sure. But then what happens if the children misspend it? Or if they get divorced, or go bankrupt? Simply saying, "I just want something simple," doesn't mean your wishes should be carried out in a simple way. Doing so provides you no protection.

However, don't worry. There are plenty of methods to help protect your assets and ensure that they reach the intended destination. In this chapter we'll go over the three main arrangements that should be considered, regardless of the size of your estate, in order to achieve this.

10.1 Beneficiary Protection Trusts

As we mentioned earlier, the first and most straightforward form of protection is a Beneficiary Protection Trust (BPT). Like all trusts, these are a legal vehicle designed to capture and hold assets, in this case usually to pass them down to your children. Assets can be passed into the trust in three ways:

- your Will instructs that the assets should be held in the BPT for your children
- you make a gift in your lifetime into the trust, setting the children up as the beneficiaries
- via a deed of variation. This is when some unexpected inheritance comes into your family from a recently deceased friend or family member; rather than having the money fall into your own estate, you vary the Will so that the money goes into the BPT.

Since the trust technically 'owns' the assets, it means that it protects the inheritance from a whole range of possible situations. For example, you might want to give your first daughter - who is married - £20,000 to help her buy her first house, so you pass it into a BPT with her as the beneficiary. She would leave that money in the trust until she was ready to buy her house. That way, should she get divorced or go bankrupt, the money is protected because your child doesn't actually own it.

With a BPT, usually both the parents and the children are set up as the trustees (assuming the children are responsible and won't withdraw the whole lot immediately), which allows the children to choose how they spend their money while still providing them protection.

Of course, this protection only lasts until the assets are taken out of the trust, which is why we always recommend that, rather than withdrawing the trust money itself, our clients instead take a loan from it. Essentially, by loaning the money out, it remains the property of the trust, and so all the protection the trust offers is retained. For example, since a loan counts as a debt against your child's estate, not as a credit, the money loaned would not be included in the financial disclosure form for divorce. Their spouse would have no claim on it.[13]

There are other things possible with a BPT, but they are certainly a powerful tool in protecting inheritance; around 90% of our clients have one. The only downside really is the cost of setting it up, which in our opinion is negligible compared to the protection that it affords, and the amount of money that could be potentially saved by using one.

10.2 Discretionary Settlements

As we saw in Chapter 7, one of the most flexible and powerful kinds of trust available is the discretionary settlement. These can be set up in many different ways for many different purposes, but a common use is to protect your assets from being inherited sideways out of the family after your death.

---

13 There is a caveat to this: if it can be demonstrated that the child was taking out a loan deliberately as a way to deprive their spouse in anticipation of a divorce, then it probably wouldn't work.

You might wish, for example, to gift some or all of your estate to your spouse, but as we saw in Chapter 9 this can lead to many problems.

To avoid these, you would set up a discretionary trust, allowing your spouse to benefit from your estate, but keeping all the assets within the trust. This would provide a similar level of protection as the BPT, in that - should your spouse remarry - the new husband or wife would have no claim over the money in the trust, because it's owned by the trust. They would have to be a named beneficiary to lay a claim.

The trust deed could then specify that, after your spouse's death, the beneficiaries should be your children. This would then provide protection to the next generation as well. As long as the assets remained in the trust they would be safe from outside claims and erosion (assuming you have chosen your trustees well), and just like a BPT the beneficiaries could take out a loan from the trust rather than the actual capital.

One type of discretionary arrangement is the family trust. The idea here is that you write out a detailed set of guidance notes for the trustees to follow after you're gone. Although it's usually preferable to create a trust in your lifetime so that you retain control, with a family trust you are able to lay out your wishes very specifically, so it is as close as possible to being able to control your assets from the grave.

As an example, we set up a family trust for a very wealthy client several years ago; unfortunately their only child, a daughter, had a drug problem, and despite many attempts at rehab it had never really worked. The daughter was set to inherit £6m, but of course if she had received all that money the consequences would have been disastrous. As the parents grew older they realised they had to plan for their daughter's future following their own deaths.

They set the family trust up so that she was named as a beneficiary, along with a couple of her cousins, and the trustees were given a long guidance note on how to handle and distribute their assets. It essentially said that the money should be used to buy property for the daughter to live in, and to give sufficient money to her each month to meet her day-to-day living expenses, but that money should only be released on the condition that she was not currently taking drugs. She had to take a regular drugs test to prove that this was the case.

Although this was obviously a tragic situation, it's clear that the family trust protected not only the parents' estate, but also their daughter's life, and setting one up can be a good way of protecting your assets from the grave, as best you can.

10.3 Life Interest

The third kind of protection is called a life interest trust. These trusts are created by the Will (so the trustee is the executor), and can be quite restricted in how they can be used; they can't collect assets during lifetime, they can't collect gifts. They are solely for collecting a part of the estate on death. However, for the right purpose they can still provide powerful protection.

Let's say a situation arose such as the one described in Section 9.4: you leave your house to your husband, with the intention that it should go to your daughter when he dies. If he then remarries, your house could potentially go to the new wife. Or if he falls ill and needs care, your property could be used to pay for that care, because it's his.

One way to avoid any such issue is to create a life interest trust in the Will. When you pass your house into the trust, the trust retains an interest in that asset throughout the lifetime of your husband, so that when he dies the asset passes to the named beneficiary (in this example your daughter). He has the right to live there, as the tenant, for his entire life, but technically the trust owns the house, not him. His lack of ownership bypasses all the issues surrounding remarriage and long-term care.

However, there is a drawback to this kind of trust. The named beneficiary, your daughter, has a right to the house. That means that if she were to get divorced, her husband could lay a claim on half of the proceeds of that house. He might even be able to demand the money immediately so that your husband would have to move out and the house be sold. Lifetime interest trusts, then, while useful in some situations, are less comprehensive than some of the other options we've discussed.

As you can see, not only are there many problems and pitfalls but there are also many different solutions that you can legally employ to make the life of your family better, both from a financial point of view and from the view of improved organisation. You have worked your whole life to build what you now have. Don't let it be lost or squandered away by improper planning. If it took 50 years to build up your assets, they are probably worth spending a few thousand pounds and 50 hours of your time on to protect.

4

PART

The Practicalities

Chapter 11

Who, What, When & Why?

We have worked with hundreds of families over the years who are left to pick up the pieces after a loved one passes on. The death of a mother, father, wife or husband, brother, sister and, perhaps worse of all, a son or daughter can have a devastating impact on those left behind. It's hard to know the best way to help everyone; death and all that comes with it are such sad and personal experiences. But we've been working with individuals and their families since 1990, and the entire team are constantly using our experiences and our expertise to find new ways of making life that little bit easier for them.

One thing we have learnt is that we can only work with the information and the circumstances we are given. If no preparation has been done and a death occurs, there's only so much we can do at that point and the families left behind suffer far more than they have to, trying to pick up the pieces. Above all else when it comes to death, both for the individual and for their loved ones, there is absolutely no substitute for preparation.

Preparation makes a huge difference to both the practical, tangible matters and the intangible emotional side of things. This is so important, we've actually written a book on the information in this section alone[14]. Helping you to prepare properly, no matter what your age, it is what this section is all about.

So what do we mean when we say you should prepare for both the practical, tangible matters and the intangible emotional side of things? What happens when you die and how do you and your family practically prepare for it? We'll then move on to your wisdom and knowledge in the next chapter. The wisdom you have amassed in your life is the real wealth that you pass down. It's what your children and grandchildren will remember you for, and it's how you can continue to guide them and help them through life, even after you're gone.

Both sections give you tasks to take on, exercises to do and jobs to complete. You may not want to do them. It is an emotional task and it's also, after all, your life (and death!). But most reading will complete at least some, if not all of the exercises in this book and we urge you to try and do the same.

When someone dies there is often so much to do, and very often we find that people are not in the right state of mind to deal with it. This is especially true if the deceased is a parent, spouse or someone close to you. It's important to step back and take a breather in these situations. Though things have to be done in a certain order, most of them don't have to be

---

14 The Life Book by David Batchelor, 2014

done right away, and it's at times like this that people make the wrong decisions.

There is an old army adage which says, "prior planning prevents p**s poor performance," and never was anything more true. But good planning can also help minimise stress for those involved, or even protect them altogether. While you won't be around, taking care of the practicalities in advance will make the process much easier for your family to manage. As we go forward, try to think of how you or a parent might feel when someone dies, and think about how you should begin to prepare to make things easier for everyone.

For example, imagine you did indeed die an hour ago. What are the answers to the following questions:

- How does your wife or husband know or find out?
- How do your children know?
- What are you in the middle of that will come to a halt?
- Does anyone know where your Will is?
- Who has access to the bank accounts?
- Who knows what funeral you want?
- Does anyone other than you have the keys to your safe?

These are all practical issues that will need to be dealt with and, unless you plan for them, your family's life will be more complicated and difficult at a time when they are emotionally vulnerable.

11.1 Communication

In the event of your death, communication is key, certainly in the first week. Letting the right people know will make your family's life easier. If you pass away at home or in hospital, we would hope that your family will be near and will know what has happened. However, if you should die when no one is expecting your death, perhaps due to an accident or some other surprise event, you need to control the information process as far as is possible.

To do this you must make sure that the authorities know who to contact. This can be done by means of either a simple piece of paper in your wallet or purse, or through an ICE number in your phone. ICE stands for In Case of Emergency, and the emergency services can usually access this without going through the entry code on the phone.

The important point here is to decide how you want people to be told, and by whom, and make a record of this. More importantly, tell your family this is what you are going to do. When you do this they will no doubt accuse you of being morbid, but that's ok – it's still the right thing to do. So try to decide who should be told of your death and when, and who you want to tell them. Tell your family about your wishes, and write it down and place a note in your wallet or purse, or record this in the ICE section in your phone.

You will also have to decide who is going to be the executor of your Will. This is a critical role, so give it plenty of thought. Ensure that the person(s) you select is not only capable of completing the process effectively, but they are also sensitive to their emotional responsibilities. Remember, they can only fulfil their role as well as your preparations allow. Taking care of the practical side of things before you die will help them a lot, so let's look more closely at some of these considerations.

11.1.1 Training Your Executors

One of the biggest errors that people make when dealing with an estate on death is to immediately pass it to a solicitor to deal with. In some cases this is a wise move, but in cases where there has been careful estate planning, this can cause terrible problems. The main problem is that most solicitors are not specialist estate practitioners, and they simply do not know the intricacies of how an estate might have been prepared. It's like going to a GP to have a brain tumour operated on.

There are times when you need a specialist, and particularly a specialist who has the ability to work with you, with compassion and understanding. There are a number of situations in which we definitely recommend clients do not try to "do-it-yourself". While the following list is not exhaustive, it does cover most situations where we think professional help should be sought:

- When the estate is insolvent
- When a beneficiary cannot be contacted
- When someone will challenge the Will

- If there is a life interest in the Will
- If any beneficiary is below the age of 18
- If any beneficiary cannot inherit at 18
- If the deceased owned a business, agricultural property or was a partner in a business
- If the deceased was a Lloyds Name
- Where the Will passes any assets to a trust or creates a trust
- If any property owned is unregistered
- If inheritance tax is payable and there is no cash or National Savings with which to pay the debt
- If a significant number of gifts were made in the 7 years prior to death
- If a beneficiary wants to vary their inheritance
- If any assets are held overseas

In any of the above cases, it is very easy to make a mistake. Also, the time involved in learning what you need to do is so great that there is little point. For this reason, choose your executor carefully, ensure that they are fully aware of the process to be followed, and that they have access to all of the necessary information required to see this process through smoothly.

11.2 Where Are The Documents?

To start, you're going to have to make sure that the executor has all of the necessary documents to apply for probate. You would be surprised how often people neglect to ensure that executors and family members have access to key documents, including the Will! The executor will also require all documents relating to your assets (and debts) so it's a good idea to organise these and keep them in one place. In terms of documents relating to your assets, this might include:

- The home (residential)
- Investment property
- Savings in bank accounts
- Stocks and shares
- Other investment assets
- Interests in absolute or interest in possession trusts
- A business, or shares in businesses
- Vehicles
- Jewellery
- Chattels
- National Savings
- Life insurance
- Pension lump sums

In terms of debts, this might include:
- Water rates
- Telecom bill
- Subscription TV
- Electricity bill
- Gas bill
- Credit cards
- Loans or overdrafts
- Mail orders
- Council tax
- Income or capital gains tax

Collating this information will be the most work-intensive for the executor, and so you can help immeasurably by recording your assets and any debts you may have, and providing them with the official documentation. If these records are in storage, make sure that the executor is aware of where they are being stored. One other crucial document is your medical card, which your family will need to officially register the death, along with the death certificate.

Of course, it's not enough for executors and family members to know where documents/items are being stored, you have to ensure that the relevant people know how to access them, and that they are authorised to do so. Make sure that someone has access to secured items such as your bank account, any safes or security boxes, and passwords.

Someone in your family will need to have keys to your home, and someone will have to know the pass code for any alarms that you may have. Make sure your house insurance details are easy to find or, better still, give the details to your family so that they can call the insurance company immediately on your death. The basic point here is to be clear on where key documents are being stored, identify who is going to have access to them, and ensure that they have all of the information that is necessary to access them.

11.3 Security

One of the biggest issues when someone dies is the security of their home. If you leave a surviving spouse this is not much of an issue, although some action will be required. But if you lived alone, the security of your home is a big problem. The problem arises from two related issues.

First, your home will be empty, which leaves it open to the dangers of burglary, especially if you died in hospital. If you died in hospital then a significant number of people will not only know that you have passed away, but they will also know your address, and that your house is now empty. Whilst 99.99% of the people you will come into contact with are honourable, and have no intention of robbing the deceased, unfortunately a small proportion may see this as an opportunity.

The second issue to watch out for is home insurance. When you take out a home insurance policy it will have a stipulation that the property can be left unoccupied for only a short period of time (usually 30 days). If the property is empty for a longer period, then the insurance can become invalid. In the event of your death, this would mean that the insurance becomes invalid at a time when there is an increased risk of theft and an increased chance of accidental damage (burst pipes, for example).

11.4 Insurance

There is one other very significant practical point, which is that a deceased person cannot hold an insurance policy. Therefore, any home insurance in your name may be invalid in the event of a claim, regardless of how long it has been unoccupied.

It may seem unjust, but we have seen situations in which insurance companies have refused to honour a widow's claim because the policy was held in the deceased husband's name.

Or perhaps this is just what you would expect of most insurance companies! It is possible to prepare for this when writing your Will, by including a clause that allows the executor to take over the existing insurance policy to cover the property.

Other practical measures to enhance security after your death will be to ensure that someone in your family has keys to your home, and knows the passcode for any alarms that you may have. And, if it there isn't a clause included in your Will, try to make sure your house insurance details are easy to find, or, better still, give the details to your family so that they can call the insurance company immediately in the event of your death.

11.5 Who You Gonna Call?

We have helped many family clients through the difficult and distressing process of dealing with the death of a spouse or a parent. There are many things that must be done and, because of the way that the legal and tax system works, these can often take many months. Other issues are more immediate, and are also more amenable to control. Two of these are the question of organ donation, and the funeral. While they seem straightforward, it is best to eliminate any uncertainty about your wishes.

Day 1

If you wish to donate your organs, this process will begin on day one. Note that in the UK you are not automatically enrolled on the Organ Donor Register. In the event of your death, a specialist nurse will check the register. If you are registered, the nurse will speak to the family about the decision to be a donor, and to ascertain that you hadn't changed your mind.

So if you wish to donate your organs, it's a good idea to register well in advance (why not today?), and to let your family know. In addition, you will be issued with a organ donor card, which you can carry with you in your wallet, and in case you are in an accident.

Week 1

The funeral is what everyone thinks about next. Arranging it is also the first formal action that your executor, family or representative will need to take. There are a number of things for you to decide. If you are like most of us, you will probably have determined whether you want to be buried or cremated, and you will have set this out in your Will. The issue here, though, is two-fold. First, your Will does not contain the details about your preferences for the funeral, and second, it will not be read prior to the funeral anyway.

We know that talking to your family about what you want to happen at your funeral never comes across well, no matter how you discuss it. So we suggest you don't. Instead, we recommend that you think about how you would like your funeral to be. Who would you like to speak? What hymns would you like sung? Should there be a reading? Should everyone wear black, tie-dye, or rainbow colors? So just think about funerals that you have attended – what went well and what didn't? This really will be the last chance you have to have a say in things (other than in your Will) and so it deserves some thought.

Of course, thinking about it isn't sufficient. Be sure to put your thoughts down on paper and keep it somewhere your family will find before they have made decisions for you. Perhaps tell them where it is, even if you don't tell them the details at this stage. In doing this you are taking a weight off their minds. You are setting out your wishes so that they don't have to make decisions, and alleviating the potential for differences of opinion, which they will warmly welcome when the time comes. So any guidance you can give will help immeasurably.

Week 2

This is where you now have to start on the real job of probate. Probate has two parts. The first is dealing with the submission to the probate office to obtain probate (probate is a document that allows you access to the estate so that you can collect it and distribute it) and the second deals with paying the inheritance tax, and will involve dealing with the IHT office in Nottingham. Until inheritance tax is paid probate will not be approved.

It is as this stage in week two that you should establish if you need help. If the estate meets any of the above criteria you will need to obtain the help of a specialist. The problem comes from the fact that you probably don't know a specialist! Why would you, when you've most likely never dealt with probate before. The best place to start is to get a referral, and perhaps the most effective way of doing this is to ask your friends on social media. By putting a question out on Twitter or Facebook you'll most likely get a lot of feedback. The main alternative is to actually meet with a specialist and see what you think.

When doing this you must consider price. Firstly, NEVER use someone who charges a percentage of the estate. The value of the estate has nothing to do with the complexity of the work. If you pay a percentage you will always over pay. We recommend that you obtain a fixed fee arrangement. When doing this consider three things:

1. The work to obtain probate.

2. The work after probate to meet the disbursal require-ments and moving assets into and out of any trust ar-rangements.

3. Who will run the trust arrangements if there are any in place.

We recommend engaging someone only for the first stage and agree a set price for this. Once this is complete you will have a good idea of whether or not you want them to continue to undertake the second and third stages. These should again be for a set fee.

Remember, a set fee is NOT an hourly rate - it is a fixed agreed sum. With an hourly rate they can simply work slowly and charge more. Why should you be charged more if they work slowly?

Chapter 12
Your Knowledge & Wisdom

The real wealth that we pass on to our family is not monetary. It is the wisdom that we develop from the knowledge we gain and the events that take place in our lives. Some people say, "some you win, some you lose". But isn't it better to think, "some you win, some you learn"? This is the importance of wisdom, and your wisdom is the most valuable thing that your family possesses. It's what they'll remember you for.

Unless you capture it, your wisdom will be lost forever and all the "wins" in your life that have made you who you are will be lost. All of your "learning" experiences will be meaningless because no one will know about them. It is these intangibles that this chapter has been designed to capture. This little section is also found in our Life Book, and is something that our clients are so happy they've had the opportunity to be reminded to do. We hope you enjoy completing it as much as your family will enjoy reading it.

12.1 The Family Tree

This is different to the family tree we talked about earlier, used to value your estate. This family tree looks backwards, and tells the story of your ancestors.

> **❝** I remember one project in particular. I would have been 10 or 11 years old and I was given the job, by my RE teacher of all people, to prepare a family tree. Of course, I was not particularly interested – as most children aren't at that age – and so I didn't take it very seriously. I met with both grandparents, who were still alive at the time, and asked them about their parents, brothers and sisters, and grandparents. At that age my writing was even more illegible than it is today, and so the resulting information that I used to prepare my simple little family tree was incomplete and full of errors. I was awarded a grade C– for the work.
>
> I thought little more of family trees until two years ago when I visited my parents and met, for the first time, one of my mother's cousins once removed. Mum had never had any contact with Chris, but he had found her when he was completing a family tree on my maternal grandparents' side. As we talked he told me the story of my great-great-grandfather.
>
> My great-great-grandfather, John Milsom, died in the late 1800s. He had been a drunk and poor husband to my great-great-grandmother. They shared a single room on the second floor of a house in Wales where they lived with their daughter (my great-grandmother). One evening John returned home both drunk and

angry. My great-great-grandmother was home with the baby, and was three months pregnant with their second child. John, known for being a foul man, argued with and beat my great-great-grandmother.

The argument took them out onto the landing, where John tripped and fell down the stairs, breaking his neck in the fall. As he lay at the bottom of the stairs, my great-great-grandmother stood there and watched the life pass from him. She made no call for help, no call for a doctor, and to be honest I don't even know if there was such a thing as an ambulance in the town at the time. But, through her inaction, John Milsom died that night. Some said this was a good thing – he was such a horrible man. But a good thing or not, my great-great-grandmother was tried for his murder.

During his work on the family tree, Chris had recovered death certificates and, more importantly, a cutting from the local newspaper at the time. The newspaper reports the incident as I have retold it here. It also reports that the judge, who was singularly responsible for deciding my great-great-grandmother's fate, found her not guilty of John's murder, nor of his manslaughter. He ruled that she was entirely innocent.

When I was 11 years old, I knew nothing of these events, and until two years ago I was equally ignorant of them. But clearly these events are profound in the history of my family. If I had known about them I would have worked harder on my school project, and would like to think I would have achieved an A+ for my work, rather than the paltry C–. But I didn't know of these events because my grandparents did not know about them. Of course, my grandmother may have known and chose not to mention them, but I don't think that's the case. I think she was also ignorant of them.

Perhaps it is my advancing years that have made these events, and my family tree, more meaningful to me. Perhaps it is the fact that my father is very ill and finds it difficult now to recall family details and events that makes our family history more important to me. Whatever the reason, my family tree is indeed important to me.

But in my busy life, running Wills & Trusts and Solidus, as well as lecturing and public speaking around the world, and as a father, putting these details down on paper is not my priority. And, although I am interested, I do not have the time to do further research. However I have supported and encouraged my aunt to do just that; she is working on the Batchelor side of the family tree.

I know that my daughters and my son will get to know all about where they came from, and that makes me feel good, knowing they'll have these stories to tell their own children one day."

David

Some people find completing a family tree an interesting and rewarding occupation. But for most, genealogy is not top of their list of priorities. Most people have busy lives, whether working or retired, and have not undertaken the work that is required to develop a family tree. We are not suggesting you spend a great deal of time on your family tree unless you want to, but we are suggesting that you take time to give it a go for your family.

It may be that your family has no interest in who came before them, but in our experience that's rarely the case. A simple family tree will be valuable in showing who they are and where they come from. And you never know, you may be helping a grandchild, a great-grandchild, a niece or a great-grandnephew to get an A+ in their school project one day.

12.2 Lessons From Your Parents & Grandparents

The vast majority of us will remember those little sayings, rhymes and proverbs our grandparents would teach us. They sound funny when you're a child and they fade in your memory as you grow up and eventually reach old age yourself. You probably have some of your own now that you hope your children and grandchildren cherish and tell their families. This is why we always ask people to think about all those pieces of wisdom and advice that they learnt and wish to pass on to their families after they're gone.

❝ I was not particularly close to either of my grandfathers. Grandad Batchelor was a carpenter who lived in Mitcham and I saw him perhaps once a month at most. Grandad Milsom lived in Putney and, because of the distance, I saw him maybe three or four times a year. However, Grandad Milsom was very close to my brother. They would play cards whenever they met and, because of their joint love of cricket, they would often go together to watch an England test match during the school holidays.

It may have been guilt about spending so little time with me that encouraged him to take me to France. The trip to France was just for one day and it was the only occasion on which I ever spent any time with him. But during that day I got to know the man as I never had before. I was only 16 at the time, and the trip was a reward for completing my 'O' levels.

We travelled by ferry and spent the day in Calais just walking around and talking. I recall we had a nice lunch, because I was allowed as many chips and ice cream as I wanted, and I recall two pieces of advice that he gave me.

Grandad was not a profound man. As far as I could tell, he had not led a particularly interesting life. He was an accountant for the local council and spent his days doing what council accountants do, whatever that is. He didn't have any great stories from the war, as I remember hoping he would. I knew he had been injured, but he refused to talk to me about it.

I later learned (from Chris's work on our family that I mentioned above) that Grandad was in the Royal Marines. He was injured during training when he was shot in the bum by another conscript, and so he never left our shores. Perhaps he was too embarrassed to tell me this himself?

However, he did tell me that he started his career working as an accountant at the head office of Lyons' tea rooms, near Charing Cross station, where he worked for several years before joining the council.

Over lunch he told me that, as far as he was concerned, there were just two things you needed to do to be successful. These were:

"Always have clean shoes", and,
"Always be on time"

Now, I'm pretty certain there is more to it than that. But I think this must have had an impact on me, not just because my shoes are always clean (which they are, before you check next time we meet!) but because I have always been fastidious about timekeeping. I've always believed that if you're on time then you're late. This has stood me in good stead and has meant that I have probably captured opportunities that I may otherwise have lost.

You might know that the first four years of my working life were spent as a professional drummer, mostly working in West End shows as a pit musician. The majority of my musical studies were conducted at Kingsdale College, where I played in the military and dance bands. Four of us always competed for the best drumming parts and, as I was the youngest, I was definitely not the best player. Consequently, I frequently got the second or third part – which is fine in a military band but in a dance band it means just turning the music for the drummer (if you watch the film Whiplash, you'll see what the reserve drummer does).

My first experience of playing at the Edinburgh Festival was as the reserve drummer, which meant that I set up the drum kit, the music and just watched the main drummer play. However, for our third performance, Michael, the lead drummer, was late.

As I was always early I took over the number one spot because Michael was not there for the warm up and "top and tail" (this is where you play the start and end of a number and check the "geography" of the part). The first piece I played in public was a Count Basie tune, called Splanky and Count Basie has since always been a hero of mine.

So, did I get the opportunity to play with the dance band at the Edinburgh Festival as a result of my of grandad's advice two years earlier? I don't know. But if I did, he was responsible for a very important event in my life."

David

Take some time to think about your parents and grandparents. Think through the time you spent with them. Think about the stories they told you of the events in their lives. Did they ever give you advice? Did you learn something from them? Maybe it wasn't anything so profound, but good common sense you realised was right once you got older.

It may take some time for the events and memories to come back to you, but ask the questions and your mind will find the answers. And when it does, capture them for the family. Write them down in this book, using the template in Appendix 2, so that they are there for the generations to come. You may not be here for the occasion when these lessons benefit someone else, but they will benefit someone, at some time.

12.3 Your Story

" "Five years ago, I started a new business venture which failed. It was called the Memory Vault. The concept of the company was that we would make documentaries of people's lives. The concept was good and we made several documentaries, but we could never make it work because the costs were too high. With a full film crew, interviewer and producer, we could not compete with people filming using simple video cameras.

However, in preparing for this failed business, I completed a one-hour documentary on my parents and their lives. I learned incredible things about my parents, which changed the way I saw them because of the renewed respect I had for what they had achieved. I particularly remember the story about their first home.

I was just three years old at the time and my brother just born. My mother had to take my brother Paul for a hospital check-up and I was left in the care of Great-Aunt Mazi for three or four hours. Now, Great-Aunt Mazi was a very distinctive character who was prone to using very colourful language – the type that would make an army Sergeant blush.

On their return, Mum and Dad had a cup of tea with Mazi to thank her for her help. While they were having tea, I put on my shoes. My mother reports that, after several minutes of struggling, I shouted "I just can't do up these f*cking laces". Sometimes we can learn things very quickly, and the profanity that Great-Aunt Mazi had used clearly had an immediate impact on me. That day, Mum and Dad decided they needed to move away and buy their own house.

My grandparents lived in council houses and it was a big deal in the mid 1960s for someone to buy a house. Nonetheless, my Mum and Dad decided this was what they were going to do. New homes were being built in Croydon and were being sold for £5,000. They needed a £500 deposit to buy one. To save the deposit, Dad worked seven days a week and moved to piece work, where he got paid based on what work he did, rather than receiving a set wage. This was a risk, because if anything happened to him he would not be paid; but if all went well he could double his income.

Mum took on home typing, which she did in the evening when Dad returned from work. Over the course of 18 months or so they saved around £400. The money was held in the Surrey Building Society. You may remember in those days that there were many banks and building societies, and also that there was no such thing as the FCA, the Financial Ombudsman or government guarantees. Unfortunately, things didn't go well because the Surrey Building Society went out of business. Mum and Dad lost all their savings, the savings that had taken a massive amount of work and effort to build.

Can you imagine how they must have felt? I'm not sure I can, but what I do know is that rather than thinking of themselves as victims, giving up and going back on the council housing list, they decided to work even harder and save even more, because it was about self-reliance rather than having an entitlement mentality. This was just one part of my parents' story. Just one part of what made them who they were, and so it is one part of what makes me who I am!"

David

You might think your story is of no interest to anyone. You might think that you have nothing to tell, but you would be wrong. Your family have an innate desire to know where they have come from and part of this is knowing you and your story. How is it that you got to where you are? How did you meet your husband or wife? Why do you live where you do, and how did you make the decision? Why did you decide to work where you work and what did you do? What made you decide to have children when you did, and what was your experience of being a first-time parent?

These, and many other things, are of real value to the next generation and the generations to come. Just think how much it would have meant to you when you were younger to know your parents' or grandparents' real story. How valuable would it be to know why they made the decisions that they did? How much deeper would your connection be to them, knowing more about them? You can use the questions in Appendix 3 to write your own story.

12.4 Lessons In Life

There's a little book called Life's Little Instruction Book that you can buy in many book shops in the UK. In 1992, H Jackson Brown decided to write a note to his son Adam, who was going to college. What began as a short note very quickly increased in size dramatically as Brown set out the lessons he had taken from life and wanted to pass on to his son.

These lessons were not long, deep or meaningful. They were usually just a line or a paragraph about something Brown wanted Adam to know. Life's Little Instruction Book has 511 different pieces of advice!

When we ask clients about the lessons they have learnt in life, most initially fail to come up with an answer. It can be tough to answer questions about what you have learned because it is so ingrained in you, in the way you think and the way that you act. We so rarely take the time to think about our own thinking. We are often so wrapped up in our daily lives that we don't have the opportunity to think about bigger things.

Whatever it is that you have learned is personal to you. It doesn't mean other people have to agree with you; it doesn't mean that others must act on it. It is simply what you have concluded about your life and the way in which you live it. Sharing this with the ones you love is deeply important. It's important because rarely do we have such conversations with people – rarely do we get to have such conversations with ourselves, let alone with other people. We've included some questions to get you started in Appendix 4.

12.5 Values

Values can be defined as the broad preferences concerning appropriate courses of actions or outcomes. Your values provide an internal compass, pointing you towards decisions about what is right and wrong. Your values determine your priorities, and are a huge part of your personality. When the things that you do and the way that you behave match your values, life is usually good and you are satisfied and content.

Your values exist, whether you recognise them or not. They have been built up over many years as a result of your experiences, what you have achieved and the things that you have witnessed. Sometimes you will have made conscious decisions about your values – what to believe – but for the most part your values will have been generated by your unconscious thought processes and filed away in your mind, from where they direct your actions and affect how you interpret the world and your place in it.

When you objectively identify and define your values you can ensure that your life more effectively follows a path that supports the things you value. For example, if you value family over work, then working a 70-hour week will not be in line with your values and will make you unhappy. But, if you value providing a sound financial base for your family, then working 70 hours may support that value, and make you feel that you are achieving something in the right area.

In his excellent book The Seven Habits of Highly Effective People[15], Dr Stephen Covey explores values and their impact on our lives. In particular he talks about value-based decisions. By this he means making decisions based upon your deep-founded values and beliefs rather than on the temporary outcomes and external influences that may be driving an event.

An understanding of your values is useful for you but it is meaningful for your family. We talked earlier about how money can change people, especially in your absence when some people may no longer feel they have anything to feel guilty about. Imagine the difference it could make if after your death, during probate, and for relations going forwards, your loved ones have the benefit of knowing your values. Knowing you'd

---

15   The Seven Habits of Highly Effective People, Dr Steven Covey, 1989.

taken the time to write those values out for them, with as much care as, or even more than, planning your estate.

Imagine years after you're gone and a child or grandchild you are so close to now has to deal with difficulties in their personal life, such as divorce, or challenges in their professional life, like growing a business. During times in life where values are so important, writing down your values now and sharing them with those who may need your support even after your death is a way for you to still be there for your family and remind them of what's important, and possibly, why certain things happened they way they did during your lifetime.

We've included a list of the most common values identified by the individuals we've worked with in Appendix 5 along with a worksheet; it may help to shortlist the top seven to ten values you see on that list, and work out from there. We've also included a section on advice in Appendix 6. After considering everything in this chapter, you may be wondering what else there is to write! But advice differs from life lessons, stories and values because it is specific. Advice is the answer you give an individual when they come to you about something that's troubling them. Advice is really your secrets to a good life.

This chapter is most certainly not easy going! But these are all the things we can forget when we're wrapped up in the practical and planning aspects of estates planning, yet they're the most important. We want to give everyone we work with the opportunity to remember to do these exercises and even though it may be hard or emotional and at first not everyone wants to, we've never met anyone who's regretted taking the time to do it.

5

PART

Post Death

Chapter 13
Prior To Probate

The submission of probate will usually take place in the second month after death, if all of your record keeping has been completed well. There is no point in rushing the probate application process because if assets or debts come to light following submission the process will need to be started again. It is always better to get it right the first time.

This book cannot cover all the details of probate application - that would probably be a 700-page book in itself, and once written it would immediately be out of date. However, it should be the job of your estate planner to help your loved ones through the process if they want help, or to leave them alone if they prefer to deal with things themselves.

If at the end of 100 days probate has not been submitted, there is something wrong somewhere. It may be that your assets can't be identified, or that your pension provider is not returning calls or letters, or any number of other things. However, if you have prepared for the inevitable by completing the sections in this book, everything should go smoothly. When the necessary preparations have been made and you understand the practicalities surrounding your death or the death of a loved one, the application for probate should be relatively straightforward.

As we covered earlier, the probate is the process that you need to go through in order to prove the estate, and to identify who is going to benefit from the estate. This section of the book pulls together some of the practical preparations, such as valuing your estate, from earlier chapters. While it can be straightforward, there can also be a lot of forms to fill out, and which ones depend upon the circumstances of the deceased. Appendix 1 shows a flowchart of the complete Probate Process to give you an overview. This chapter will cover the main things you need to consider prior to probate.

First of all, the estate gets summarized and sent off to the probate office. Then the probate office will assess the summary of the estate, look to see if there is any tax liability, and request that any such tax is paid. If there is no tax liability, or once the tax has been paid, they will then provide the executors of the Will with what's called the grant of probate. The grant of probate then gives the executors of the will permission to distribute the estate.

It's important to ensure that everything is in place to facilitate this process, and to be clear on how to proceed when the time comes. The previous section laid out some of the practical considerations, and this chapter covers the steps you'll have to take prior to probate.

13.1 Registering A Death

It may sound unpleasant, but when the time comes someone is going to have to register your death. In England and Wales the death must be registered within five days. This can be quite tough, depending on your family situation. To be clear, registering the death is not the same as obtaining a death certificate, which will be issued by the doctor who pronounced the death. Once you have this certificate, the death must still be registered in the formal registry known as the register of Births, Marriages and Deaths. When you register a death you must take with you:

1. The death certificate (unless the doctor has sent this directly to the registrar)
2. The deceased's NHS medical card

Registering the death starts the process of notification to the relevant authorities, and is absolutely essential for dealing with all the various product providers, right down to having your Will released from your chosen storage facility. It's a simple process, but one that you need to go through.

Essentially, you will have to notify anyone you can think of that the name of the deceased is on an account with. So, bank accounts, BT, Sky, utilities, other subscriptions. Whoever it is that's going to want to know that that person has died.

There are two basic reasons for this. First of all, they'll want to make sure they don't ring up and ask for Mrs Smith when in fact she's dead, because that's not a nice experience for the person taking that call and it makes the company look and sound insensitive and out of touch. Second of all, it will enable them to ascertain whether there is any tax due on the account (if applicable), as they would have to notify HMRC of that. They will also ask you to produce a death certificate.

Though it may seem insensitive, they're not doing anything out of the ordinary when they make that request. Asking for the official death certificate is part of a process for a lot of companies and is in place to prevent fraud or other errors. You just have to be prepared for that.

13.2 Valuing Assets

Before probate can be applied for, whoever is dealing with the estate must know what the estate consists of. This sounds simple, but just like our list of documents noted above, it can be difficult to establish if you have not recorded what you own, and where it is. In order to establish the value of the estate, two main things must be identified. The first of these are the assets, and the second are the debts.

Hopefully you completed the assets and liabilities exercise in Chapter 2. In doing so, you're making it easier for whoever will be dealing with probate to sort out. Having an up to date, complete list of all your assets and liabilities could save them weeks if not months of work. If you've yet to complete that exercise, you can find a list of common assets as well as the exercise itself on page 22.

When your estate's being valued, absolutely everything you own is being taken into consideration. For example, if you've got property, then a valuation would be needed. Generally, the rule of thumb is invite three estate agents round.

They'll give you an estimate of the market value of a property, and you can select the middle one. Ideally, you want it to be on the lower end of things if there is going to be some inheritance tax to pay. But, if we're being squeaky clean, then you go with the middle one. If you adopt this approach, there can't be much of a dispute with regards to the valuation.

Other things that need to be valued are investments and bank accounts. With both of those, the valuation may fluctuate. For example, you may have a bank account where interest is added, or you may have investments where the value fluctuates on a daily basis. What you're looking at is the valuation on the date of death. If you haven't contacted the bank or the investment company for a week or two after the day of death, they will be able to look back and give you a valuation on that particular date. And that's what is important.

13.2.1 Joint Assets

Valuing individual assets is relatively straightforward, but you'll need to provide information on any joint assets as well. If there are joint assets, you need to assess whether those joint assets were split on a 50/50 basis, or whether there was a defined split. There are two ways of owning most assets: 'joint tenancy', and 'tenancy in common'. Joint tenancy means they own it together, and legally the asset has to pass to the other party.

So, supposing you own a house in joint tenancy with your wife. If you die, it has to pass to her.

Regardless of the fact that it has to pass to her, from a probate perspective, the estate will be valued as if you owned 50%. In the case of a tenancy in common, then each co-owner has a distinct share of the property and is entitled to leave it to whomever they wish after they die.

13.2.2 Debts

It is critical that you do not overlook any outstanding debts. When you're looking at the valuations of everything, and you're trying to determine whether there's going to be a potential tax liability on the estate from the inheritance tax perspective, you need to make sure you've got a true valuation. All the figures we've talked about up to now are going to give you a gross figure. What you don't want is the probate office looking at that gross figure when you've got half a million pound mortgage elsewhere that's going to net down the value of the estate. So in conjunction with ascertaining the value of any assets, and who owns what, you also need to look at the debts.

What debt did the client have in the event of their death? Are those debts still there and do any need to be paid by the estate? With something like a mortgage liability, that's almost certainly going to have to be repaid unless it was joint names. In such a case, the debt is going to pass to the spouse or partner.

On rare occasions, credit card bills are written off, so they will actually die with the individual. However rare that might be, it does happen. You hear stories of people racking up credit card bills prior to their death in the hope that that will just be written off when they die.

It's best to think of such instances as a PR strategy, rather than as an act of corporate benevolence. If you're a credit card company and someone has £1,000 debt, and you then drag their widow through the courts trying to get that money back, it doesn't look too good. It only takes the local media to get wind of the proceedings. And in this day and age, especially with social media as well, all of a sudden a huge household name gets a bad rap for being mean to an elderly person. A lot of the time it's just easier for them to wipe the slate clean. But don't count on it!

13.3 Inheritance Tax (IHT)

By now we should have completed the summary of the estate. We've looked at the valuations. We've deducted any outstanding debt. Using these figures we are now going to be in a position to declare net value. Though it's one most people would rather skip, the next step is to calculate whether there is any inheritance tax liability on this sum.

13.3.1 Calculate

It's the responsibility of the executors to initially calculate whether there is any inheritance tax liability to be paid. There might be no tax to pay, if the value falls within the nil-rate band (i.e. the normal allowance that they can pass down without any tax liability), or if it's a first death scenario and the deceased is passing everything to a surviving spouse. There's no tax to pay between husband and wife, but most other cases are not so straightforward.

Before you are able to determine whether IHT is due, you take the net value of your estate and deduct any available allowances. If there's a nil-rate band available for the individual, it needs to be deducted from the estate. If they're the second to die and they've been married previously, you will have to determine if there was any of the nil-rate band available to carry forward from the deceased person, or if they had already exceeded the threshold.

13.3.2 Payment

In terms of the payment of inheritance tax, probate will not be granted until any tax liability has been paid. This means that if there's £500,000 inheritance tax liability on an estate, it has to be paid first before the beneficiaries can receive their inheritance. This is one of the main reasons that so many people are concerned about inheritance tax. In some instances, people will come to us and say they want to avoid paying altogether.

When Gordon Brown was Chancellor, we'd have people coming in and saying, "I just don't like that Scottish guy and I'm not going to give him my money". While at times this has its roots in political affiliations or ministerial antipathy, some people just don't want to pay the taxman. Others will state that they just want their kids to get as much as possible, which by default means that they don't want to pay the taxman.

The necessity of paying this tax upfront is one of the main reasons that people want to avoid inheritance tax liability. If beneficiaries could just inherit the money and then pay the taxman, it would probably cause people much less concern. Of course, from the Inland Revenue's perspective, that's a big risk because people might well inherit the money, run off, and never pay the taxman at all. In fact, that used to happen all the time. While the system can cause problems, there are a number of other funding options available to beneficiaries.

13.3.2.1 Funding

Strictly speaking, it's the executors' responsibility to pay the tax, and if the beneficiaries are likely to struggle to pay the tax in full themselves, there are a number of funding options you can put into place. Firstly, the executors can make an application to the probate office to allow them to access specific bank accounts from the deceased estate. So they can say, "Joe Blow over here has got a Quest bank account with £100,000 in it. You can take the first £100,000 of the inheritance tax liability from that bank account". There are only specific companies that allow this to happen, but if you can load up bank accounts it will save your beneficiaries having to find all the money.

The problem is no one knows when they're going to die. It doesn't make financial sense to hold all of your money in a bank account, not knowing when you're going to die. You don't get any interest from it at the moment, and it could be years before the kids actually need it and have to pay the tax liability.

As a second option, we might have put some kind of life

insurance in place. In such a case, the life insurance might be available to pay the tax liability. If you do have life insurance policies in place, and those policies have been ring fenced by trust arrangement, that will pay out immediately. That is, within a matter of days. You don't need to wait for probate on that side of things because it's an asset that's excluded from your estate.

So if you're worried about the kids having the money to pay the taxman, you can put life insurance in place to provide them with a lump sum when you die. It's not the most sophisticated way of dealing with inheritance tax planning, because essentially you're funding it yourself through insurance premiums. You're never going to pay as much in premiums as you would eventually be paid out. But, still, it's not the most sophisticated way of dealing with it.

13.4 Collection

When it comes to the collection of the estate, it's best to think of it as one big melting pot. Clients tend to try to compartmentalise their estates. So they will say, "That's my house. That's my money. Those are my investments." They think this is what they're passing down to their beneficiaries but all they're passing down, realistically, is the value of those things. Over time, the executors are going to sell off all of those assets. They're going to sell the shares that you've got. They're going to cash in the life insurance policies.

They're going to sell the property. Once they've got all that money in the big melting pot, they can then start thinking about how to distribute it going forward based on the wishes within the Will.

13.4.1 Outstanding Tax

Before distribution, there's the question of outstanding tax to be paid. This is not inheritance tax, but existing tax from the deceased's estate. If someone were to die on April 5th, at the beginning of a new tax year, then all their taxes would probably have been paid already. The problem is, most people can't time it like that! So what happens if you die part way through a tax year? There's always going to be some tax that was due. It could be income tax that was payable from your salary. Or it could be dividend tax that's payable from some share holdings. Interestingly, Capital Gains Tax dies with you.

All the other tax liabilities, however, such as income tax, tax on interest, dividend tax, carry forward and the estate has to settle it. This could also include tax on interest that's been earned between the day of death and the day the assets cross over to the beneficiaries.

Outstanding tax has to be paid. As part of the probate process, you will also have to declare the death with HMRC so they can do a calculation of any tax that's going to be due up to that particular point. And again, that's all the responsibility of the executors. If there are no executors, and if they've died without a Will in place, then the personal representatives will be responsible.

13.5 Grant

Once you've collected the assets, and you've paid any outstanding debt, including the inheritance tax side of things, the probate office are then going to provide you with grant of probate. The grant of probate is a physical document which is like a certificate that basically says: this person has died, and this was the valuation of their estate. That's important. We'll come back to that in just a moment. The grant of probate gives permission to the executors to begin executing the Will, i.e. distributing the assets, and carrying out the wishes that have been enclosed within the Will document itself.

It's always important that the assets aren't distributed too early. Imagine, you've collected up all the assets that you think the client has, and then all of a sudden, six months later, there's this dividend payment that comes through from BP. And you think, "Well I didn't know he had BP shares". Now, if you've already distributed the estate and you find that there's another £100,000 worth of BP shares, you're going to have to go back to HMRC and recalculate potential inheritance tax liabilities, which might in turn alter what each of those beneficiaries would receive.

Most of the time, this isn't an issue because probate can take months and months. The fastest ones, the really simple cases might only take about three months, but the more complex ones can take years. If it's a really complex case, or if the application falls in winter when there are generally more deaths, it might take a long time for the probate office to process things and get the estate summarized.

As a general rule of thumb, most dividend payments come out every six months, if not a shorter period, so it's probably a good idea not to distribute the assets for at least six months. By chance, most probate cases will take at least six months anyway. It gives you that breathing space to make sure that anything that might come through, like dividend payments, has already come through. You know exactly what the estate is.

13.5.1 Accounts

Finally, it goes without saying that it's vitally important that the executors keep good accounts of things. For example, what was the house valued at? What did you do with that money? What we tend to recommend is that they open up an executor account, in which they can receive all of that money as and when it comes through. This will give you the final account in which to store the inheritance, which can then be distributed to the beneficiaries. To facilitate this process, the account side of things should probably happen quite early on. Someone should open up the account in the name of the executors for the deceased estate so that things can be collected up and handled effectively, and transparently.

Now that you've been awarded the grant of probate and have an account in place to handle the inheritance, we can move on to consider the post probate process.

Chapter 14

Post Probate

In an ideal world all of your careful preparations have paid off, the executor has moved seamlessly through the application process, and the probate has been granted. Once the probate has been granted, we can move on to the post probate side of things, which is the physical disposal of the assets. While this stage is relatively straightforward, there are a couple of points to consider. Here, we first reflect on the implications of your decisions with regard to the human side of the process, which is too often overlooked. Next we provide some notes and clarifications on beneficiaries, and the disposal of the assets.

14.1 Human Side

One of the most important bits when it comes to someone dying is family. The sad fact of the matter is that money changes people. We've seen it many times. The preceding chapters covered practical considerations, and the things that you can put in place to make life as easy as possible for the family. While this is a great start, it's worth bearing in mind that the biggest issues often arise when there isn't an equal split on an estate. Straight away, this risks causing a rift between family members.

> **"** "Sadly, my grandmother passed away early this year. Whenever anyone mentioned anything about Wills or inheritance to her, she would talk about when her mother-in-law died. This was many, many years ago. She would recall how everyone came to the house and took what they wanted, and how her sister-in-law took a rocking chair that had been promised to my mum. We're going back 50 years here. And it was a chair. It had no significant value and it wasn't written down anywhere that my mum would get it. But it still stuck in her head. And it was still a big issue between her and her sister-in-law. She had a lovely life, and was married for 70 years. Why let something like that bother you? But, it definitely can."
>
> **Dean**

The human side of your preparations is making sure that you don't leave behind those kind of niggles and hassles. This can be really difficult. It's not easy to know what people would want to take, and what you should leave to certain people. What we always say to people is, if there is going to be an unequal split, justify it in some way, shape or form. Not that you should have to. What you do with it is entirely your choice.

But let's say you've given £80,000 to your daughter, and £50,000 to your son. Perhaps have some form of letter of wishes that your executors can read through and then explain to the son, "You are only getting £50,000 because you spent most of your life living at home, rent free with mum making the bills and washing up for you. That's why the daughter got a little bit more. Because she up and left home a long time ago." Explaining things in this way can help avoid these rifts, but an uneven split is always likely to cause tension between the beneficiaries.

14.2 Beneficiaries

The beneficiaries will typically be defined in a Will. They can't pick and choose. If the Will states that a beneficiary is to get a third of the estate, that beneficiary has to get a third of the net estate. If it states that a beneficiary is to get a specific book, that beneficiary has to get that book.

There will usually be a 'power of appropriation' clause in most Wills, which basically allows a beneficiary to say to an executor, "I don't really want this book. I'd like to have £10 instead". Then the executor would have to ask the other beneficiaries, "Do you want this book instead of your £10?" So it is possible to negotiate. Again, it's best just to try and keep things as fair and even as you possibly can do.

It could be that the beneficiaries are under the age of 18, or the age stated in the Will. Often people will allocate a portion of their estate to grandchildren, but specify that they are only to inherit that money when they reach the age of 21. In such a case, those assets are held in a trust. This can be relatively simple, if you think about it like a bank account. If you've got kids, you hold a bank account in their name because they're too young to manage it themselves. Technically, that is held in trust. It's not your money; you are entrusted to look after that money for that individual up until they reach a certain age.

14.3 Disposals

Disposal of the assets should be relatively straightforward. If you have created the executor account, you will have a pot of money and a Will in front of you which states how it should be divided up. In the really simple cases, it will be an equal share for all beneficiaries. In the case of beneficiaries who are minors, or under that stated age within the Will, the executors become their trustees. So the executors will be responsible for managing the money for those beneficiaries until they reach an age where the assets can be disposed of i.e. distributed to that beneficiary because they've now reached the age of 21.

If there is a specific bequest in a Will, such as a specific book, or an item of jewellery, the item has to be valued. When you're drafting the Will, it is important to take that into consideration. Do you want someone to inherit your ring, for example, which is valued at £10,000?

Do you want them to inherit it without any inheritance tax liability? In that case, it has to come out first, before the tax liability is calculated. When we're dealing with clients, and we're talking to them about those things, you have to explain the negative kind of effect that those gifts can have. If you've made a lot of gifts down at this end of your Will, it's going to have an effect down the line.

Suppose that, before we get to that big melting pot, you've

given away a grandfather clock, a picture, and a necklace, and that the value of these gifts amounts to a £100,000. That comes out first, and it comes out without any inheritance tax paid on it. That means there's going to be a negative effect for the people at this end. They're going to have to pay the tax. Because the tax on the estate is not dictated by who inherits it, excluding spouses, obviously. If it's anyone other than a spouse, then there's going to be a tax liability. So you have to make sure that this is all taken into consideration.

PART

Successful Estate
Planning

Chapter 15

The Estate Planning Scorecard

You've covered a lot of information over the last 14 chapters, and while we've tried to simplify it as much as possible, we all know it's not exactly easy reading! So well done for getting this far. To wrap up this book and to help you create your next steps, we've created a scorecard you can use to easily determine what skills and knowledge you already have that will help you plan your estate successfully, and what skills and knowledge you could employ to make the task ten times easier.

It's a way of assessing how you might apply what you've just learnt and will highlight any areas you may need additional support in, so that when you sit down with the Financial Adviser of your choice to go through your estate, you can let them know where you feel confident and where they may need to provide you with further guidance or information.

Over the last 25 years, having helped hundreds and hundreds of individuals successfully plan for what they want to happen after they pass away, we have noticed there are certain characteristics that people who are good at estate planning have, and those who are bad at estate planning don't have.

There are eight characteristics in total and we'll expand on each of these now, before giving you the scorecard to complete yourself. The scorecard measures your views towards the 8 characteristics listed below.

15.1 Vision

What we tend to find is that people are typically at one of two ends of the spectrum when it comes to vision. There are loads of people who have a very clear idea, and probably a recent idea, of what they want to achieve and how far they have to go to achieve it. They are often diametrically opposed to those people who are not sure of what they want at all. They're not sure of what they've prepared and they don't understand the relationship between short term pain and long term gain, so they find it hard to make much progress with their Wills.

The reason why not knowing what you want works against you when drafting a Will is that if you don't really know what you want, you can't verbalize it or be clear about it, which halts discussions with an Adviser before they've even begun. Also on the spectrum are the people somewhere in the middle. They know what they want, but they're not prepared to do anything about getting it. In financial terms, you cannot save half a million pounds of tax by paying £3.50, or just doing well. Some things are more complex.

You have to accept that if you want to legally reduce inheritance tax, protect the assets for your children and legally make sure that your assets don't get split up in divorce of a child, then you've got to take some action and actually take some fairly drastic action, both with regards to the establishment of various legal tools but also with regards to being prepared to make changes to your own circumstances and estate.

We'll sometimes have a discussion with a client where we'll say, "You're going to need to transfer your house into a trust," and it's just too big a jump for them. They'll have an inheritance tax bill of half a million, yet they don't come to terms with the fact that they've got to make some changes and perhaps they've got to incur some legal fees.

If you're reading this book thinking you want to reap the benefits we've outlined using the strategies we've discussed, it is the role of the Adviser to judge which exact strategies suit your personal situation but your responsibility lies with creating a clear vision of what you want. The easiest way to create a clear vision is to get really specific and quantify your wishes. For example, rather than simply state that you don't want to pay any tax, write down what you do want, both for you and for those you care about who you'll leave behind. A good, clear, concise vision includes what you are prepared to give in order to achieve what you want.

People who do estate planning properly tend to have that vision, although a large portion of people just don't. Vision is probably the most important characteristic.

15.2 Family

The second characteristic of good estate planners is they have a good sense of family. They're very clear about their family.

They put plans in place correctly and set things up properly. They understand they can't take the money with them and they have a deep understanding of what would happen to their family when they inherit, and they know who's going to get what and when. They really think through scenarios such as, "What if my children suddenly get a million pounds each; how would that impact them? Will it change their lives? How will it change their lives? If so, how should I give them the money and when should I give them the money?"

People who are very poor at estate planning are unsure about who should inherit and when. There also tend to be many disputes within the family that make it difficult for them to make decisions. Probably 50% of the families that we deal with have circumstances that are not straightforward. Rarely do we come across a family with 2.4 children and everybody's happy. There's always something in a family that will cause an issue with a Will and the more complex the circumstances, the more complex the arrangements that they need to put in place.

Those who are successful estate planners have this deep sense of family and understand the importance of how making arrangements will change the family both positively and negatively (because sometimes inheriting at the wrong time can be a negative factor).

15.3 SKI-ing

People who are good at estate planning tend to be very good at SKI-ing. Not skiing on snow, but SKI; Spend the Kids' Inheritance. They tend to have a structured plan to spend their money so that they can die poor. People who do good estate planning should die poor. You don't really want any money when you die. It makes it much easier to ensure it goes to the right person if you pass it during your lifetime. It's much easier to avoid tax if you have no money when you die.

SKI-ing is a good thing for estate planning and that means understanding when you can gift assets during your lifetime, which is obvious ly the best way to avoid tax. If you can give everything away and then live seven years, that's by far the best option. It's always the cheapest option, but you've got to make sure the plan works out well because you don't want to run out of money. Usually they have a plan to die poor but they overestimate what they need to live off and they never run out of money.

That means turning an estate plan into a broader financial plan. It means your investment strategies, spending strategies and taxation strategies should reflect on the estate plan. It all comes as a whole. This isn't something that can be done independently. All too often, we see people who want to pass everything down to the children and avoid tax, yet their financial plan is all over the place so it's difficult to even identify what they've got, where it is, and how it can be moved.

It makes the job of the person doing probate and dealing with the practicalities much more complicated. You've got to know where everything is; you've got to find everything. The number of times we've come across people who have done some form of estate plan themselves, yet no one can even find where all the documents are is dreadful. SKI-ing is all about making sure that you get rid of everything to make life easy for everybody concerned.

15.4 Decision-Making

Another common characteristic of those who are great estate planners is the ability to make decisions. In order to have everything planned out properly and die knowing life will be as easy as possible (from a practical perspective) for your loved ones as well as avoiding tax, you've got to make spending decisions and you have got to make big, long term decisions, such as transferring your house into a trust. You have got to spend money but if you're a bad decision-maker, you might feel too scared to spend it or move it. People that won't make decisions will find it almost intrinsically difficult to do any form of estate planning.

15.5 Growth

What we mean by that is growth-orientated people have a growth mindset and continually increase the value of their estate, and that's always likely to carry on happening. We've talked about how passing gifts to other people can affect their views towards personal financial growth. Generally, people who are good at estate plans tend to be quite good about understanding what personal growth means.

If you have someone who doesn't care about growing and changing personally, financially, intellectually or otherwise, they are unlikely to put a good estate plan together because they're not thinking about bigger issues. Growth is quite a nebulous one. It's intangible but it does affect people.

15.6 Taxation

Your view on taxation impacts how good you are at putting an estate plan together. If you believe that you have the right to pass on what you own to whomever you want to, without taxation, and you believe you've paid enough tax when you earned it so it's unfair to be taxed further, you will likely go further to make sure your assets go to the right person rather than going to the chancellor. These are people who would say, "I've paid income tax when I've earned it, I've paid VAT continuously, I've paid income tax on all my earnings, why should I then pay tax on assets that I've got leftover?" Those people tend to actually take some action.

However if you believe that it's wrong to inherit from your parents, or if you believe that what you inherit reduces your ambition and makes you lazy causing an entitlement mentality, you may not be very good about making estate planning choices. A person's view on taxation will have some impact upon how they go about doing their estate planning.

15.7 Being The Boss

People who are good at doing estate planning tend to be people who will take action and take charge. Too many people defer the decision to somebody else, for example, "I've got to discuss this with my wife; my children; my accountant; my solicitor." As blunt as it may sound, we've learnt that that's simply an excuse for indecision. Those people that make decisions and take charge, they are the boss. They are the ones that tend to be very good at doing the estate plan, whereas those people who are continuously second-guessing and take ages cause a problem. Not because they do anything intrinsically wrong but because they over-think things. People who are the boss will always do better from an estate planning point of view.

15.8 Peace Of Mind

People who consider peace of mind the objective tend to do very well from an estate planning point of view as well. They want to sort everything out and put it all to bed. Everyone says they want peace of mind but few are actually prepared to do something about it, and too many people say it and don't actually do anything. They swear they'll get around to doing it yet rarely do. People who genuinely want peace of mind tend to plan very well.

15.9 The Ambition Scorecard Exercise

If you struggle with estate planning, or if you're new to it, use the scorecard overleaf to figure out where you stand on each of these eight areas. If you're a four, that's great news! If you're a one, two or three, that particular skillset could do with some development and focus to make your own life easier (and cheaper).

Vision	You are not sure what you want or what you are prepared to do to get there	You know that you want to pay less tax and who is too benefit when you die but have done little to understand how to achieve what you think you want	You have thought about what you want but think writing anything down is tempting fate. You have shared and discussed very little with your family	You have a very clear and written idea of what you want to achieve and are prepared to go to any lengths to achieve it
Sense of Family	You are unsure about who should inherit and when. There are many disputes in the family that make it difficult for you to make any decisions	You are pretty sure who will get what and when, but you have done little more than write a Will, and are unsure if this is up to date. You have given little thought to how your family will deal with what is left to them	You have a loving relationship with all your family & are keen to make sure that they inherit the right amount at the right time so that their families are strengthened by your legacy	You know that you can't take it with you and have a deep understanding of what would happen to your family when they inherit from you. You know who will get what and when
Peace of Mind (Doing the right thing)	You get tied up in the detail of things and want to check everything yourself. You worry about making decisions and keep revisiting decisions that you have made	You are prepared to consider alternatives but are often worried that you don't know enough to make a decision	You focus on the result rather than the detail. You always focus on the bigger picture, giving you a greater sense of calm and confidence	You want to know that everything is in place so that you don't need to think about it again. Making life easier for your family is key to you. Detail is irrelevant as you always delegate it to others
SKI	You know that you need to spend more but are scared that you might need it, so much so that you rarely make a decision which is difficult	You are spending more than your estate grows but it is unstructured and frivolous. You still often get worried that you will not have enough money when you get old	You are spending a reasonable amount on yourself and your family but it is adhoc and reactive and you still feel guilty about what you are doing with your money	You have a structured plan to spend and use your money so that you die poor, passing little onto your family because you have already given it away or spent it

Growth	There is little prospect in the value of your estate growing. Even your home is likely to be used to pay for care that you might need in the future	Your estate will grow but is unlikely to outpace inflation. You are likely to spend what comes in so your net estate will probably stay the same forever	Your estate will continue to grow no matter how much you spend and there will be too much left when you die which will cause problems on your death	The value of your estate increases continuously but in such a way as to avoid increased tax problems. Whatever your family inherits will be protected for them in the future by structures you have put in place
Taxation	You believe that it is wrong to inherit from you parents and that if you inherit it reduces your ambition and can make you lazy and have an entitlement attitude	You feel that tax of your estate is reasonable to help those less privileged. You believe that the government use the money they collect from you wisely	You believe it is reasonable that some tax should be paid when you die, but that the levels that your children will pay is too high, and so you should take action to reduce it to a more reasonable level	You believe that you have the right to pass what you earn to whomever you wish without taxation. You believe you have paid tax when you earned it so it unfair to tax it a second time
Being the boss	You believe that as your children will inherit, they should deal with issues as they arise and meet any costs that might be involved. You care little for taking action when it comes to tax planning	You want to get the full story before making a decision and want to discuss this with every 'stakeholder'. You rarely act without the unanimous view of your family and advisers	You are able to consider all relevant issues and make decisions. You listen to others' opinions, and use them to come to a confident decision based on advice	You make the decisions. You are good at listening to experts and seeing the bigger picture. Once you have made a decision it stays made.

Chapter 16
Next Steps

So, how did you fare? Are you someone who's going to do something today, or will you become one of the majority who leave a complicated situation behind and give lots of tax to the chancellor? Are you going to take action, provide for your loved ones after you've gone and get that peace of mind, or will you read the book and let the information float around in your mind as unresolved questions?

Our goals for writing this book are that you feel better educated on the core principles surrounding estate planning and that you feel equipped to start making decisions. Now is the time to ask yourself: do you know what you want, do you know who's going to get what you want, and are you prepared to let somebody else help you to do that?

If that is the case, then we recommend that the Adviser you choose to work with has both the ability and your trust. Those are the two most important criteria. Do they have the ability, the knowledge, the experience? Some clues to look for when evaluating potential Advisers is how long they've been doing estate planning for (at least 10 years), and how many clients have actually passed away whose estates have gone through the processes of the inheritance tax office and the probate department. A minimum number you'd want to hear is at least 50. That's because it takes that much experience to really know the process inside and out. If they don't, then their ideas could be just that; ideas.

What will help you the most is proven processes and results. You also want to work with someone who has the ability both from a technical point of view, but also from the point of view of being able to express and share that information with you so that action can be taken. If an Adviser/solicitor/lawyer can't explain concepts and ideas in ways you can understand then it's going to be a futile effort on both parts.

So ability is very important. Trust is also important because everything you agree, draft and plan for is going to actually come into fruition following your death, so you've got to trust that the people you've selected know what they're doing and will follow things through in the ways you want.

David's dad always said that people have a nonsense meter that goes off if they think something isn't right. Well, he used a slightly different terminology than 'nonsense', but you get the point! The point is if you don't have 100% confidence in the person that you're working with or the team that you're working with, then you should question whether you should use them at all.

Another point worth considering when it comes to trust that's important to understand is that it's all well and good relying on one person, but what happens if something happens to that person. You want someone who's part of a team so that if they're not available for whatever reason (they may die themselves, or move on to another firm), the team will carry things forward. It's not just about having a person you trust but also having a company that you trust. A company with the right values that works with people who are similar to you.

One way to assess this is to find someone who's already working with them. A testimonial is by far the best way of checking because that's the only way you're going to find out what a service provider is really like.

Most estate plans should take anywhere from three to nine months to put into place. If it can be done quicker, that could suggest it's not being done properly. Unless your circumstances are extraordinarily complicated, you should expect it to take three to nine months to put it into place. Subject of course to everybody involved playing ball. For example, sometimes it takes time to get approval on various aspects of a trust, or sometimes it takes a long time to get your trustees to sign the relevant documents, which may slow things down. There could be some outside circumstances but by and large three to nine months is what your time range should be.

One thing we want to prepare you for is some understanding of the variables that impact the cost of having someone do your Will. When we say cost, we mean both the financial cost and the cost in terms of time and complexity. Some cost is inevitable; as we've discussed, doing your Will yourself is a bad idea. But it's important to know that the bigger the problem, the bigger the cost.

If someone's got an estate worth £5m and they want an estate plan putting together for it, that could and should be reasonably straightforward. It should also be massively expensive, because if you've got an estate that's worth £5m and you've got a tax bill of £2m you've got to accept that you'll be paying some of that. It's likely that you won't understand exactly how it works so you've just got to trust the person. It always comes back to trust; you have to trust that they know what they're doing.

You probably have plenty of questions after reading all of this and going through the exercises, so thank you for doing so. In taking the time to read and digest the information in this book, you've taken the first step towards having the Will that you want, that will best provide for your family after the inevitable happens. In following the guidance outlined, you now have enough knowledge to vastly decrease the complexity of your Will, and therefore the cost, and can choose an Adviser to work with knowing how they should be supporting you and what your and their responsibilities are when it comes to your estate planning.

If you'd like to contact us with any thoughts, questions or comments, we'd love to hear from you and are happy to help: http://www.wills-and-trusts.co.uk/

Glossary

7-Year Rule PETs fall out of the estate after 7 years. Before this they are subject to tapering tax relief on the value of the gifts.

Ambulatory Document Before death a Will is a living document, subject to changes in circumstances and legislation; the law at the time of death applies, not at the time of writing the Will.

Assurance Trust Used to avoid inheritance tax on life insurance at second death, by setting up the trust as the beneficiary of the insurance, rather than the spouse or children.

Beneficiary Individual who receives a part or the whole of the estate as directed by the Will, or assets from a trust.

Carry Forward If you are married or in a civil partnership, the percentage of your nil rate band that was unused (due to the spouse or civil partner exemption) will transfer to them as a percentage of the current nil rate band at second death, so that the two nil rate bands are combined.

Cy-près Doctrine   Element of UK law allowing the executor freedom to pass on a charitable gift to a similar charity, should the named charity no longer exist.

Disbursal Trust   Created on death by the Will – an administrative tool to collect all the estate together into the trust of the executor (now also the trustee) until the assets can be distributed.

Discretionary Settlement   A trust where where the trustees can make certain decisions about how to use the trust income, and sometimes the capital. Can be used to avoid inheritance tax on second death.

Equalisation Clause   A clause in the Will to ensure that all beneficiaries take their proportional share of the estate, taking into account gifts made from the testator in their lifetime.

Executor   The person nominated by the testator to oversee the distribution of assets as laid out in the Will after death; assets pass into the executor's care in a trust immediately on death, so this person should be chosen wisely.

Gift And Loan Arrangement

A trust for financial investments in which the settlor retains full access to the original capital (which remains in his or her estate), but any growth on top of this falls into the trust rather than the settlor's estate.

Guardian

Legally appointed by the Will, the guardian is given parental responsibility over any minors left without a parent.

Intestacy

The condition of the estate of a person who dies owning assets without having made a valid Will - the law dictates where their assets should go, but if no valid recipient comes forward the government will claim the money.

Letter Of Wishes

A non-legally binding letter laying out your intentions to the executor, to clarify issues that might not be covered by the Will.

Lifetime Chargeable Transfer

Gifts made during the lifetime into (most kinds of) trusts which, after 7 years, no longer count towards the estate for inheritance tax purposes. They are not subject to tapering tax relief.

Master Trust	A trust that holds pension money after death, until the distribution of the pension can be undertaken as laid out by the Nomination of Benefits form.
Nil Rate Band	Once an estate reaches a certain threshold, inheritance tax is liable. The amount under this threshold is tax-free and is called the nil rate band, which in the UK is currently £325,000.
Nomination Of Benefits Form	Separate to the Will, this form directs a pension, usually into a Master Trust and then on to a named beneficiary, after death.
Pecuniary Legacies	Gifts of a fixed sum of money in your Will. The value of pecuniary legacies will decrease over time due to inflation.
PETs	Potentially exempt transfers are gifts made during the lifetime which, after 7 years (the 7-Year Rule), no longer count towards the estate for inheritance tax purposes. Before then they are subject to tapering tax relief.
Probate	Legal approval that grants the distribution of assets as directed by the Will.
Retained Income Trust	A trust which allows the settlor to retain any income made on the asset within the trust.

Can be used to avoid inheritance tax on property.

Remaindermen The second line of beneficiaries who inherit or are entitled to inherit assets upon the death of the former owner.

Remoter Issue 'Issue' means children, and remoter issue includes further generations within the bloodline that are yet to be born.

Residential Nil Rate Band First introduced in April 2017, the RNRB will, when fully implemented by 2020, provide a £150,000 tax-free allowance per person against a residential property, provided that it is passed on to your children or grandchildren.

Second Death Clause Clause in a Will directing where assets should go if the primary beneficiary dies.

Settlor The person setting up a trust.

Spousal Bypass Trust Used to avoid inheritance tax on pensions at second death, by setting up the trust as the beneficiary of the pension, rather than the spouse or children.

Testator The individual who is writing their Will.

Trustee

Looks after assets in a trust - the trustee is the legal owner of the assets in a trust that they hold for the beneficiaries. The executor becomes the trustee of your estate at the point of death; the Will creates a disbursal trust, which gather all your assets into their care.

Appendices

Probate Process

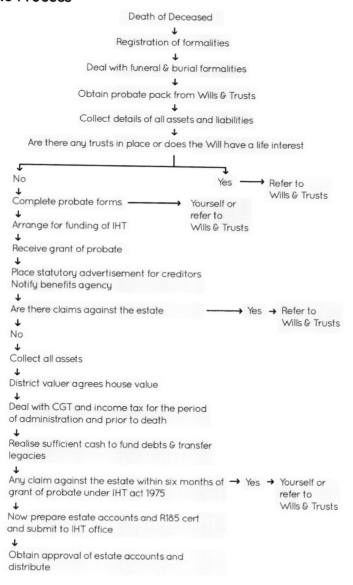

Advice

You are smarter today than you were 20 years ago. You are smarter because you have built wisdom from your experiences, both good and bad. When giving advice it's probably better to think about giving your younger self advice. Of course, you may not have listened, but think about how your words will look when your great great grandson or granddaughter read them in 20, 30 or 40 years time. Reflect on how you would have respected advice from your grandparents; that is how your family will see your advice.

What do you think about money? How does it affect the decisions you make in life and how can you advise your family to use the money they have or will have to generate the most positive results in their lives, and the lives of others?

_____

_____

_____

_____

What is important about family? How should we act towards family? Do we treat them as someone special just because they come from the same blood line or is it more about the character of a person?

_____

_____

_____

_____

How did you make your goals? Were they written down and structured or were they just in your head waiting to spring forward when needed? What would you tell your younger family about goal setting and using it in life? What books would you tell them to read?

_____

_____

_____

_____

If there was only one thing that everyone should do to make their life better what would it be? Is this something you do or have done? If you could write just one paragraph on the secret of life what would it be?

_____

_____

_____

_____

Lessons From Your Parents
& Grandparents

Please use the following questions to spark memories that will help you recall what wisdom your parents and grandparents passed to you.

What did your Grandfathers do for a living? What did they tell you about what they did, and what did it teach you?

_____

_____

_____

What stories did your grandmothers tell you? What messages were hidden in those stories, and what did you take from them?

_____

_____

_____

What do you find yourself telling your children which came from the mouth of your parents?

_____

_____

What did your parents say about your first job? What advice did they give you?

_____

_____

_____

As you think about your parents, where do you copy them? Where is it that you act in the same way?

_____

_____

_____

If your parents were to give you three pieces of advice, what would they be?

_____

_____

_____

Lessons in Life

If you could go back in time and could ask yourself three pieces of advice, what would that advice be? Why would you give it? Would you have listened?

1._____

_____

_____

_____

2._____

_____

_____

_____

3._____

_____

_____

_____

Values

Accountability
Accuracy
Achievement
Adventurousness
Altruism
Ambition
Assertiveness
Balance
Being the best
Belonging
Boldness
Calmness
Carefulness
Challenge
Cheerfulness
Clear-mindedness
Commitment
Community
Compassion
Competitiveness
Consistency
Contentment
Continuous improvement
Contribution
Control
Cooperation
Correctness
Courtesy
Creativity
Curiosity
Decisiveness
Democraticness
Dependability
Determination
Devoutness

Diligence
Discipline
Discretion
Diversity
Dynamism
Economy
Effectiveness
Efficiency
Elegance
Empathy
Enjoyment
Enthusiasm
Equality
Excellence
Excitement
Expertise
Exploration
Expressiveness
Fairness
Faith
Family-orientedness
Fidelity
Fitness
Fluency
Focus
Freedom
Fun
Generosity
Goodness
Grace
Growth
Happiness
Hard work
Health
Helping society

Holiness	Reliability
Honesty	Resourcefulness
Honour	Restraint
Humility	Results-oriented
Independence	Rigour
Ingenuity	Security
Inner harmony	Self-actualisation
Inquisitiveness	Self-control
Insightfulness	Selflessness
Intelligence	Self-reliance
Intellectual status	Sensitivity
Intuition	Serenity
Joy	Service
Justice	Shrewdness
Leadership	Simplicity
Legacy	Soundness
Love	Speed
Loyalty	Spontaneity
Making a difference	Stability
Mastery	Strategic
Merit	Strength
Obedience	Structure
Openness	Success
Order	Support
Originality	Teamwork
Patriotism	Temperance
Perfection	Thankfulness
Piety	Thoroughness
Positivity	Thoughtfulness
Practicality	Timeliness
Preparedness	Tolerance
Professionalism	Traditionalism
Prudence	Trustworthiness
Quality-orientation	Truth-seeking
	Understanding

Uniqueness
Unity
Usefulness
Vision
Vitality

Your Story

Where did you go to school? What was the best and the worst thing about going there?

_____

_____

_____

At school, who were your friends? As you remember them what were they like? Did you try to mimic them or were you always the leader?

_____

_____

_____

What made you choose your first job? What other alternatives did you have, and why did you decide against them?

_____

_____

_____

What did you learn in your early career? What would you do differently if you had that time again?

_____

_____

_____

When did you meet your spouse? What is your history, and how did you get to where you are?

_____

_____

_____

What are the three best things that happened in your life which were not children being born? What caused them to happen?

_____

_____

_____

What was the one piece of advice you wish you would have taken, if you had been given it and had been in a place where you would have listened?

_____

_____

_____

PA1 FORM   www.hmctsformfinder.justice.gov.uk/HMCTS/
GetForm.do?court_forms_id=735

IHT 205   webarchive.nationalarchives.gov.
uk/20050301194629/inlandrevenue.gov.uk/
cto/forms/iht_200ws_1.pdf

IHT 400   www.gov.uk/government/uploads/system/
uploads/attachment_data/file/497785/
IHT400.pdf

About The Authors

David Batchelor has worked in financial services for over 35 years. He started his own company, Wills & Trusts Chartered Financial Planners, in 1992 with a small £9,000 inheritance from his grandmother. David lectures around the world on all areas of financial planning, but focuses on estate planning and UK taxation. He is both a certified Financial Planner as well as a Chartered Financial Planner and was a founding board Director of The Personal Finance Society. He is a question writer for the Chartered Insurance Institute.

Dean Hobbs started his business life with Britannia building society before moving to Wills & Trusts 15 years ago. Dean is a registered Financial Planner and specializes in estate and tax planning. Dean is a speaker on estate planning issues and gives presentations to both the public as well as training financial advisers both in the UK and the USA.

David and Dean have worked together for close to two decades in their practice Wills & Trusts Chartered Financial Planners, and are in demand as trainers to Financial Advisers who are keen to move onto advanced tax planning.

They have authored this book now to help those who are currently looking to plan their estate and take care of their families after they're gone, but do not have an understanding of what's involved and the resources available. Supporting people through what can be a challenging and emotional process is at the heart of what David and Dean do, and the number one reason they consider this book to be so important.

Printed in Great Britain
by Amazon